The
Good Society

COMPASS PROGRAMME FOR RENEWAL

The
Good Society

COMPASS PROGRAMME FOR RENEWAL

Edited by
Jonathan Rutherford
and Hetan Shah

in association with
Lawrence & Wishart

London 2006

Lawrence and Wishart Limited
99a Wallis Road
London
E9 5LN
www.lwbooks.co.uk

Compass
Southbank House
Black Prince Road
London SE1 7SJ
www.compassonline.org.uk

First published 2006

Copyright © Compass 2006

British Library Cataloguing in Publication Data.
A catalogue record for this book is available from the British Library

ISBN 1 905007 49 3

Members of the Good Society Working Group

Ash Amin	Roshi Naidoo
Valerie Bryson	Martin O'Neill
Bea Campbell	Andrew Pakes
Balbir Chatrik	Jenni Russell
Ian Christie	Mike Rustin
NiraYuval Davis	Jonathan Rutherford (chair)
Alan Finlayson	Hetan Shah
Tony Fitzpatrick	Eric Shaw
Don Flynn	Kate Soper
Paul Harman	Sukhvinder Stubbs
Gerry Hassan	Willie Sullivan
Will Higham	Adam Swift
Sue Himmelweit	Rachel Thomson
Catherine Howarth	Malcolm Torry
Nick Johnson	Heather Wakefield
Peter Kenway	John West
Neal Lawson	Stuart White
Ruth Lister	Richard Wilkinson
Jo Littler	Fiona Williams
Bilkis Malek	Rebecca Willis
Paul Miller	Christian Wolmar

All contributions were made in a personal capacity. This book aims to reflect the mix of ideas and balance of discussion that emerged, but it should not be taken to be representing the views of any particular member of the working group and individual contributors do not necessarily agree with every conclusion in the book.

About the editors
Jonathan Rutherford is chair of the Compass Good Society working group. He is editor of Soundings and Professor of Media and Cultural Studies at Middlesex University.
Hetan Shah is policy director at Compass. He was previously director of the New Economics programme at the new economics foundation, a think tank.

Acknowledgements

In addition to the members of the working group, we would also like to thank for valuable input and comments: Ed Balls, Louise Bamfield, Robin Blackburn, Alessandra Buonfino, Joanna Collins, Martin Cooper, Anna Coote, Lynne Friedli, Sue Goss, Daniel Harris, John Harris, David Held, Daniel Hodges, Martin Hyde, Daniel Leighton, Roger Levett, Ruth Levitas, Mahua Nandi, Howard Reed, Steve Richards, Gita Sahgal, Polly Toynbee, Jon Trickett and Andrea Westall.

Particular thanks to Sally Davison at Lawrence and Wishart for managing the production and publication of the book.

Thanks to the Joseph Rowntree Reform Trust for providing general funding to Compass.

Thanks also to the Barry Amiel and Norman Melburn Trust, Unison, and the following Compass members for providing financial support for the Programme for Renewal: Rebecca Allen, Jack Andrews, Keith Barnard, Victoria Barr, Barbara Barrett, Tony Belton, Clara Bentham, Roy Bentham, Paul Blomfield, Jeffrey Boss, Philip Bradley, John Bull, Joseph Buttle, Margaret Camina, Philip Carter, Peter Cawley, Sarah-Jayne Clifton, Julian Coman, Jeremy Cooper, Paul Cornick, John Crisford, Mike Cuddy, Hugh Davies, Marilyn Evers, Geoff Garrett, Dan Godfrey, Alan Goodfellow, Miranda Grell, John Grieve Smith, Megan Griffith, Ian Hancock, Ryan Heath, David Higgins, Ron Hikel, Del Hosain, Norman Hunt, Alan Hutton, Martin Ignatius Gaughan, George Irvin, Martin John Holst, Philip Jones, Graham Kemp, Peter Kenyon, Maurice Line, Ruth Lister, Margaret Maden, Linda McAvan, Des McConaghy, Peter McGinty, Fiona Millar, Denis Mongon, Andrew Morton, Lawrie Nerva, Neil Nerva, Ray Newton, Wendy Nicholls, Jim Northcott, Richard Pennell, Denis Pethebridge, Anne Rafferty, Howard Reed, Fraser Rennie, Judith Roberts, Tim Roberts, John Robertson, Tony Robinson, Meg Russell, Jonathan Rutherford, Roger Sainsbury, Chris Sewell, Henneke Sharif, Eric Shaw, Victoria Silver, Peter Smith, Nigel Stanley, Jean Stead, Steve Strong, Kathy Sutton, Lindsay Thomas, Alan Tomlinson, Glyn Tudor, Bob Tutton, Giovanni Vitulli, Laurence Whitehead, Larry Whitty, David Williams, Barbara Williams, Robin Woodburn, Richard Young.

Contents

The Compass Programme for Renewal

Compass is a pressure group providing direction to people and organisations who want a more democratic and equal society.

The historic project for social justice and democracy has stalled and is in urgent need of renewal. After the failings of post-war socialism, the rise of Thatcherism in Britain and the domination of neo-liberal values and practices across much of the world, the response of New Labour has been mixed.

New Labour was a creation of pessimistic times. Now, over a dozen years since its birth, its legacy could be described as good in parts. Yes, it has humanised more elements of a rampant market than the Tories ever would have done, but, paradoxically, it has also deepened the grip of the market on society.

Crucially, New Labour adapted itself to the economic rationalism of the neo-liberal project rather than attempt to go beyond this debilitating hegemony. It has failed to break with the old ways of doing politics, and has not responded to the new threats of the market. The problem with New Labour is that it is neither new enough, nor Labour enough. It is a project that has run out of steam.

Building on the partial successes of New Labour, but also learning from its failures, it is time to think again. The Compass Programme for Renewal is the start of that process. Launched just after the 2005 general election, the programme is an ambitious attempt to rethink ideas and strategies for a more equal and democratic society. In the process it offers a space to build alliances between individuals and organisations who share the goals of Compass, so that they may over time become a reality. It is to the synthesis of ideas and organisation that Compass aspires.

The central objective of this politics is to enable people to become the masters of their own destiny. As Gandhi described, we want to be the change we wish to see in the world. Markets have an important but necessarily restricted role to play: the ability to manage our world can only be achieved by working together as citizens, not as individualised consumers.

For freedom to flourish, we need more than greater equality as individuals, so we can all live fulfilled lives. We also need the institutions and processes that will allow us to act together to manage the world around us. True choice requires the possibility that we might change the terms of choices offered to us – to want, and be able to build, a different kind of world.

There are three interlocking elements to this renewal process:

- A vision of a good society – to fuel our political aspirations
- A new political economy that supports this vision – exploring how we can become more enterprising and creative, but also manage markets for the good of society as a whole, at the same time sustaining the life of the planet
- A revival of democracy and the public realm, so that we have the capability to withstand the pressures of an over-encroaching market, and to act collaboratively to determine both what the good society is, and how to progress towards it.

The Good Society is the first in a series of three short books that form the first stage of the Programme for Renewal. They are a collaborative product of many people's time, experience and knowledge. This collaboration includes not just the input of the members of the Working Groups listed in each book, but also submissions from Compass members, findings from desk research, expert interviews, and commissioned 'thinkpieces' that can be seen on the Compass website.

The analysis offered in the books is challenging, and mirrors the threats and opportunities society faces. The policy strategies are not yet systematically formed but are strongly symbolic of a fresh, popular and achievable new politics.

The strategic challenge we face is in linking reforms that are achievable now with a process that transforms our society. The aim is not just a marginally better world, but a different one, where the values of democracy, equality and solidarity, and therefore true freedom, become the new hegemony. Power and principle are two sides of the same coin. How do we balance them effectively?

We don't have all the answers, but these three books mark the start of an overdue debate. We actively welcome contributions and criticisms, in writing or via the space for debate on our website. Compass is also taking the debate out to the countries and regions of Britain with a Renewal Roadshow. Our aim is to engage with progressive organisations and individuals the length and breadth of Britain, including MPs, council leaders, charities, social entrepreneurs, progressive businesses, environmentalists, trade unions, community leaders and think tanks. And after this we aim to conduct a similar process at the European level, in order to build international networks that make a more equal and democratic society a reality.

You can contact Compass as follows:
Website: **www.compassonline.org.uk**
Email: **info@compassonline.org.uk**
Postal address: **Southbank House, London SE1 7SJ**
Telephone: **020 7463 0633**

Foreword

We are losing the ability to imagine different ways of living. This is fatal to the future of our society. Every stage of progress starts as someone's dreams. Where would the idea of a National Health Service have come from if not someone's utopian thoughts?

Roberto Unger, the Brazilian political theorist, tells us that 'to be a realist you must first be a visionary'. We must know what we are being realistic about, otherwise we have no compass to steer us. Politics without the hope of a different world simply dies. We can see that starting to happen in Britain as the parties converge on the same territory. The absence of real choice means that the number of people voting declines, along with membership of political parties and trust in politicians. Progress is the chase for utopia. Without the chase no progress is made, and we stand in danger of slipping back.

Today we are healthier and live longer than ever; we have access to incredible technology; we understand the human mind, nature and science as never before. But our lives – depending on where on the social scale we find ourselves – are either contorted by ambivalence or wracked by poverty.

Many have experienced an increase in wealth that has not been matched by any increase in happiness. As the celebrated economist J.K. Galbraith said, 'there are many visions of the good society; the treadmill is not one of them'. We want security and personal freedom. But the two are proving to be incompatible. We have never had it so good – but at the same time we have never had it so bad.

For many others life is a grim struggle of survival. More than 11 million live in poverty in the UK. Rich or poor – all of us are more alone, more insecure and more anxious. This is because the primacy of free markets has fuelled a social recession.

Privatisation is something that happens not just to national industries, but to our own hopes and fears. Increasingly we are left with only individual solutions to the entrenched problems created by the whole of the economy and society. We cannot buy our way out of these problems, and the pressure of this harsh impossibility places an unbearable strain on all of us.

Consumerism cleverly compensates us for the loss of our collective ability to act. Like any form of compensation it provides us with rewards that we readily embrace. But ultimately it can be no more than that – compensation for a greater loss. Compulsively hunting for the next thing to buy or experience, to express our ever-changing identities, demands so much of our time – not least in hours at work to earn the necessary cash – that it leaves little energy or space to think about a different world, let alone to act.

So we are left with the tools to change everything about ourselves but not the world around us. Empowered as consumers we have become disempowered as citizens. Utopianism today is not about how we might build a better world together, but how we can survive on our own the frustrations and anxieties of a modern capitalist world. We survive through a mix of escapism – holidays, hobbies – and the fight to stay on the treadmill of consumer success.

Because we cannot take on the burden of dealing with the social recession as individuals, we must look for new grounds for hope. Growing numbers of people are experimenting with new kinds of living to create a better society. More of us are choosing to have increased time for friends and family rather than more money – and this is not restricted to the well off few. A quarter of 30-59 year olds made a long-term decision to downshift in the last decade. Eight million wore wrist bands to make poverty history, and the majority of us would support increasing taxes to end child poverty.

Record numbers of people are creating new ways to connect with others; through volunteering, campaigning, online communities, book groups or buying fair trade products. They are prefiguring a good society by improving each other's quality of life. Some of us are investigating how to lead enjoyable lives without impacting on our environment. 63 per cent of us are in favour of new green taxes to discourage behaviour that harms the environment. And it's not just people but businesses that want to see progressive change. Recently, fourteen of the biggest UK corporates lobbied the prime minister to get the government to regulate against climate change.

Greater diversity and less deference, a hunger for new experiences, more open and global minds, and new concerns such as the environment and third world debt are the foundations of a new politics. While politics nearly always lags behind the cultural curve, it is time for new optimistic political leaders to forge and maintain this latent progressive consensus. The progressive wave that swept New Labour to power in 1997 is still rolling. It is the wave that David Cameron is trying to ride when he talks about public services, the environment and now even equality and redistribution.

We have lived too long in a dark age of political pessimism. The failure to make society the master of the market disempowers us all. Unchecked markets don't just do untold damage to individuals and communities. Their elevation to become the sole means and ends of life restricts our ability to be anything other than individual economic actors. So even if we dream of a better life for our children than we had, the reality is that we are becoming the first generation to bequeath a planet that is in a worse state than it was when we inherited it.

The sociologist Zygmunt Bauman reminds us that there are two conditions for the imagination of a different world. The first is the overwhelming feeling that this world is somehow broken and needs to be fixed. The second is the confidence in the human capacity to rise to the task. A belief that 'we can do it'.

In this age of autonomy, the central dilemma is this: can the thirst to create our lives and the world around us be quenched primarily through the market, or is it greater democracy and equality that will set us free? The race is on to win hearts and minds before we lose the belief that something different is possible. The danger is that we forget what it is that we are being compensated for.

There can be no grand design about what constitutes the good society. Every vision is – rightly – different and particular. Democracy is the conversation amongst equals to determine what constitutes the good life and the good society. If utopia is the chase for progress, it's the journey that matters, never the blueprint.

For me, and I think for many others, the good society is determined by an ability to control more of my life and by definition be free of the control of others. I want the opportunity to be creative in my work and leisure, to have more quality time with the people I love, to contemplate, read, play and volunteer. I want to feel the exhilaration of being empowered in concert with others – the rush that comes from knowing what amazing things can be achieved if we co-operate rather than compete. And I want to be free of the knots in my stomach caused by my part in the destruction of our planet and the unnecessary poverty and suffering of others. I want to celebrate our joint humanity. It is because all our lives have the potential to be rich, creative and wonderful that we cannot waste one of them.

We live in good society already – it's just that it is not ours. We live in the good society of neo-liberal beliefs and practices, because they had the courage and the capacity to build it.

It serves those who benefit from this system to claim that 'there is no alternative'. But alternatives do exist. They exist as ideas in our minds that we can turn into reality. And they exist too in countries like Sweden that are outward-looking, dynamic and creative but more equal and social. Of course we cannot simply become Sweden. We have our own particular circumstances to address and build on. But we can learn the lesson of their long journey. It is the lesson of political pragmatism at its best: vision tempered but not thwarted by realism.

We are fast entering a period when we will be tested not just by our words but by our deeds. It is a moment in which we must transcend narrow self interest and become once more self-enlightened. If we fail to have a vision of the good society and the fortitude to struggle for it then we will end up with more of what we have already got – a market society. It is time to recognise again the difference between what is and what could be.

Neal Lawson
Chair, Compass

1 The good society

What is the good society? Who asks such things in politics today? We are bereft of a vision of a better life. In many ways we live in a society of unparalleled social stability and affluence. In the last three decades the size of our economy has almost doubled. In the last fifty years national income has tripled. The majority of people own their own homes, millions take foreign holidays. Supermarkets offer a cornucopia of choice. Music, books and cinema are accessible to the majority. The media and the internet provide a wealth of information, knowledge of the world and entertainment. More people study at university than ever before and science is extending the realm of human possibility. Consumerism and new technologies offer us unprecedented means for self-expression. And in our ethical life there is a greater tolerance for difference, a growing willingness to be open to the world around us.

Our great grandparents would be stunned by the plenitude that surrounds us and the richness of our lives. Many of them had to struggle with material hardship, and here it seems is the promised land. But if they surveyed our turbo-consumer society they would sense that something has gone wrong. There is a malaise that is difficult at first to identify.

Material prosperity has not brought with it increased satisfaction with life. Our pursuit of fulfilment has stalled. The relationship between economic growth and well-being has broken down in the rich countries of the world. The measures of subjective well-being which assess the happiness of the population have shown little movement in thirty years.

We have become a more unequal and divided society. Levels of personal debt are unprecedented, and we are time-poor, working long hours either to make ends meet or to buy the ever changing trappings of success. Alongside the economic insecurity a new set of social problems has emerged – widespread mental ill health, systemic loneliness, growing numbers of psychologically damaged children, eating disorders, obesity, growing alcoholism and drug addiction. The Sainsbury Centre for Mental Health has calculated that the total cost of mental illness to the economy is £77 billion.[1] Stress, anxiety and depression account for a third of all working days lost.

We are living in a social recession. Its symptoms and its pain are often concealed inside our homes, where we experience them privately as our own shameful and personal failings. Without a wider political understanding of this social recession, we have no means of understanding its causes, let alone the ability to deal with its consequences.

The principle cause of this social recession is unrestrained market capitalism, a mid-nineteenth century idea which was reclaimed in the 1980s by the Conservative government. The ideology of neo-liberalism was summed up in Margaret Thatcher's now infamous pronouncement: 'I don't believe in society. There is no such thing, only individual people, and their families'. The individual would henceforth be set free, and the size and functions of government reduced. Only the free market of 'competitive capitalism' could ensure the ending of political control over the economy, and so guarantee individual liberty from the state.

The welfare state began to be dismantled. Mass unemployment was used as an economic instrument to drive down labour costs and undermine the bargaining power of the trade unions. The liberalisation of the money markets with the 'Big Bang' in 1986 allowed an extraordinary global expansion of capital. This was aided by the privatisation of public utilities. In the phrase later deployed by Bill Clinton, it was the dawning of the age of 'the economy, stupid'.

What gave neo-liberalism a popular resonance was its claim to enhance individual liberty. The idea of personal choice, the aspiration to make a life of one's own, to no longer defer to one's 'betters' or be subjected to a paternalistic state, chimed with the post-1960s cultural values of self-expression and personal identity.

The old monolithic state had rightly become a target. But the problem with neo-liberalism is that in order to promote the market it also promotes a culture of individualism: instead of seeking to ensure the flourishing of individuals through democratic and therefore responsive collective means, it promotes only a narrow and selfish individualism. The idea of a public good or common interest is dismissed. If what holds people together are economic forces, then they need to be extended into all areas of life. Thus price – and proxies of price such as targets and performance indicators – came to displace values of association and solidarity as the means of governing and serving the people. Institutions and organisations in the public sector were reformed, to become subject to market-based criteria of economic performance.

These changes created the conditions for the social recession we now suffer. They broke apart the network of social ties and mutuality that constituted the public realm. Mass institutions, such as political parties, withered on the vine, unable to function in a world of rampant individualism. Trust in politics and many other social institutions has been eroded, to be replaced by transactional processes.

In order to impose order upon the newly disadvantaged, the state and sections of the media promoted an authoritarian morality of family values, nationalism and welfare obligations, to take the place of broken social bonds and declining loyalties. A strong state is necessary to police the free market.

This is the world that fashioned New Labour. Unable and unwilling to build a counter movement to the forces of free-market capitalism, New Labour made its accommodation with the neo-liberal times. It constructed a new centre ground, and with considerable political skill inflicted defeat after defeat on a now exhausted and divided Conservative Party. But its critique of Thatcherism was partial not fundamental. For New Labour, the failure of neo-liberalism was its denial of the role of a reformed state in making Britain better equipped to compete in a global economy. Not only was the state necessary to create order from the social fallout of neo-liberalism: it could also be harnessed to improve employability through improved education and other supply side reforms. But this renewed emphasis on the state was accompanied by measures to make it operate more like the private sector – and therefore, supposedly, more efficiently.

New Labour's electoral victories were achieved, in part, by deepening and broadening the Tories' subordination of the political to the economic. They have been willing to implement a weak social democratic agenda, but these measures have been largely undertaken in the name of economic efficiency. New Labour has achieved important reductions in poverty, and has managed to implement a number of socially liberal measures. But it has never made a serious challenge to neo-liberalism by seeking active political support for an alternative, democratic – and hegemonic – vision of the good society, because it has only ever wanted to 'modernise'. Unaccountable and unacceptable concentrations of wealth and power have therefore not only remained untouched, but have been encouraged.

Neo-liberalism has delivered a restricted and mean-spirited view of freedom. Its reliance on markets to distribute liberty has resulted in historically unprecedented inequalities in life chances. The nation state has not diminished in size: it has been transformed into a new kind of market state. No longer a provider of services, it is instead an enabler of market provision and an enforcer of market values.

Material wealth is offered as the basis of the good life by today's free-market capitalism, but this brings with it diminishing marginal satisfaction, and is paid for by a social recession. We need to challenge neo-liberalism culturally, politically and economically. This does not imply anti-capitalism, as the second book in the Compass Programme for Renewal series, *A New Political Economy*, explains in detail. Far from it. The creative power of markets can be a powerful liberating force. What is required, however, is greater social control over the destructive consequences of
free markets.

Neo-liberalism is built on a very clear and very simple conception of the human being. She or he is an individualised bundle of wants and preferences, a machine constantly calculating how best to gain advantage over others in the struggle to satisfy those desires. That is why the right believes that the only freedom that matters is the freedom of the marketplace, where the only choice is whether to buy or sell.

In contrast to this simplistic and impoverished neo-liberal conception of the individual, humans are marvellously and uniquely complex. People certainly do buy and sell to satisfy their needs. But they also create, play, love, invent and wonder. People want to go the moon not just to find opportunities for profit but because it is there and we want to know what it looks like up close. When people study and learn they often do want to obtain qualifications to increase the sale-price of their labour. But they also want to learn about themselves and their world, to satisfy their curiosity and expand their horizons. People seek economic satisfaction, but they also seek emotional and social satisfaction.

Humans are interdependent, social and emotional beings, fundamentally oriented towards, and dependent upon, other people throughout our lives. What gives meaning to our lives is our social connections to other people. Our needs and our aspirations are formed socially and we can only live together harmoniously if these can find a high level of fulfilment. A society that is not organised in line with these fundamental needs is likely to crash into a full blown social recession.

Individual freedom grows out of our interdependency, not in opposition to it. The self fulfilment of each is indivisible from the equal worth of all. Real freedom to flourish requires that we have the resources – money, time, relationships, political recognition – to live our lives with meaning. Each citizen is afforded equal respect, security and chances in life, regardless of background.

The good society values diversity – its notion of solidarity acknowledges differences of culture and identity, and is not bound by simplistic considerations of national integration. It is open to our increasing global interdependencies. It seeks to understand the meaning and purpose of life through a pluralist and inclusive ethics. In the good society the ethic of care comes before the work ethic. Human dependency and need are not marginalised, but integrated into economics and social life. Framing all these values is ecological sustainability. The good society is a part of the planet, and attuned to its ecology. It develops ways of flourishing within the constraints imposed by the eco sphere.

We live today with a public language that is inadequate when it comes to articulating the common good. But the values of a better society already resonate among many people. They are widespread in personal ethics and politics, and underpin unarticulated anxieties and moral ambivalences. They are incorporated into countless single-issue campaigns, community actions, pressure groups, voluntary organisations, cultural activities, civic obligations, and a multitude of informal individual engagements with political, charitable and social issues. The moral concerns and democratic practices of these small-scale politics provide the practical and philosophical resources for a new kind of pluralist politics of freedom and equality. Each alone is insufficient to transform and improve the material conditions of our society. There is a need for a collective politics that can bring them together, in order to create a common voice and agency.

It is still within our capabilities as a society to renew the collective and democratic impulse for freedom, equality, and solidarity. Through the struggle to achieve such a goal the good society will be born.

2 Equal and free

In order to create free and flourishing citizens, the guiding principle of the good society is social justice, the ethical core of which is greater equality. Everybody needs access to the resources to lead a fulfilling life. Individuals require equal civil, political and social rights; the means to effectively exercise these rights through the equitable distribution of power and influence; sufficient income and wealth to meet essential needs and live a secure and dignified life; an equal opportunity to achieve well-being and development of capacities; meaningful time free from employment and unpaid labour; the conditions in which their health (including mental health) can flourish; environmental security; and the recognition and respect which confers self esteem.

How far from this vision are we? The numbers of cars on the road, the crowds heading for the sun on bank holidays, the designer labels and household expenditure on entertainment and leisure, all these suggest a society of mass affluence. But underneath inequality is rife.

Free-market capitalism has created historically high levels of inequality. In the last fifteen years the number of billionaires has nearly tripled, and the number of individuals worth over £100million has risen fivefold. In 2005 an average FTSE chief executive was paid 113 times more than an average UK worker. The richest 1 per cent of the population own approximately 25 per cent of marketable wealth. A tiny but influential elite has excluded itself from society. These are the untouchables, part of a global elite who share zones of glamour and luxury. The world is made in their image as governments compete for their favour. Tax avoidance and large inheritances boost their wealth. They have no stake in the quality of public education, the NHS or public transport.

In contrast, the least well off 50 per cent of the population shares only 6 per cent of total wealth. Half of the families in Britain own assets of £600 or less. Of these, 25 per cent are £200 or more in debt. [2] While the rich elite have easy access to everything they want, the majority are paying for the relative spread of material prosperity with unparalleled levels of personal debt, which now averages £5000 per household. The reality of Middle England is not a life of ease but a median income of £21,000. Most people are just one pay cheque from destitution.

The rise in income and wealth inequality since 1980 has reversed the overall trend of the twentieth century towards a less class-bound and more egalitarian society.[3] New Labour has been aware of this inequality. It has made important reductions in levels of pensioner poverty and child poverty, and has increased levels of public spending. Commitments have been made to reduce health inequalities; reduce the numbers of 16-17-year-olds excluded from employment, education or training; and improve the employment rates of disadvantaged groups. However, to date it has succeeded only in stemming the trend towards greater inequality, leaving inequality effectively unchanged at historically high levels.

The life chances of individuals are determined by the luck of birth more than ever before. Children born in different classes have very different chances of enjoying a secure and happy childhood, sustaining good health, and achieving self-fulfilment and a prosperous later life. The inequalities created by class are compounded by discriminatory practices and attitudes around gender, race and disability. Women workers in Britain suffer one of the biggest gender pay gaps in Europe. [4] Despite legislation against discrimination, the differential outcomes across a range of areas between racial groups are still stark and pernicious. Unemployment is over one third higher amongst ethnic minority communities than their white counterparts.[5] People with a disability have a disproportionate risk of being poor.[6]

Inequality is intensified through the burden of relative deprivation, and those who start out at a disadvantage tend to experience a large number of problems associated with it: teenage births, crime, prison incarceration, poor educational performance, shorter life expectancy and ill health. Britain has the highest teenage conception rate in Western Europe, and the life chances of teenage mothers are greatly reduced by the lack of education and training available to them. People living in the poorest neighbourhoods are nearly six times more likely to be murdered than those living in the richest areas.[7]

As income and wealth inequalities have risen, social mobility has decreased. New Labour's hope of a meritocracy has failed to become a reality. One important cause is the strong link between family income and educational attainment. It begins in infancy and is institutionalised at school. A child's social background, not the type of school they attend, is the crucial factor in academic performance. [8] Over the last thirty years the proportion of people from the poorest fifth of families obtaining a degree has increased from 6 per cent to 9 per cent; the proportion for the richest fifth has risen from 20 per cent to 47 per cent.[9]

The redistribution of wealth to the rich has a corrosive effect on all classes and social groups. [10] A collective sense of security is eroded, violence increases, and individuals are less likely to be involved in community activities. People feel more vulnerable and become distrustful of each other. Fear of crime and general fears for personal safety increase. A culture of low-level anxiety, allied to personal acquisitiveness, undermines the values of social solidarity and reciprocity. Those living in poverty feel abandoned. The middle classes struggle to maintain their standard of living, insecure at work and fearful for the safety and prospects of their children. Education is turned into a competition to win access to the employment market, and children pay the price in terms of stress and, often, mental ill health. Meanwhile the rich elite increasingly inhabit a separate world from everybody else. Gated communities, private security and the increasing use of private jets and helicopters insulate them from public spaces and everyday life. Their privilege and excess corrodes the fabric of society. Governments tax less and therefore do less. Public services, often the only real solution to social ills, are further undermined. The flight from public solutions to privatised answers is exacerbated.

This is the vicious cycle of decline that fuels the social recession.

Being rich is not only a way of asserting superiority over others; it is also means to gain their esteem. Those lower down the hierarchy feel disrespected, devalued and looked down on. Economic growth that does not address inequality is not the answer. Relative income and status is extremely important, because it defines where we are in relation to others and confirms our social nature. Inequality has a profound impact on all of us.

Scientific evidence shows that inequality of status creates ill health, and this helps to explain the seven year difference in average life expectancy between men in Glasgow and those in Dorset. Life expectancy decreases at every step down the social ladder: even those who are comfortably off tend to have shorter lives than those who are very well off. Reducing inequalities will not only improve the lives of the least well off, it will improve everybody's quality of life.

Policy strategies for renewal

To achieve greater equality requires policies and institutional reforms over the long term, and spread across a wide range of social and economic relations. We need to redress inequalities relating to gender, race, childhood, ageing and disability. We need to tackle inequalities of resources such as time, work, health and care, all of which impact on the life chances of large sections of the population. In particular more effort is required to deal with the unequal distribution of social networks and social capital, which is another key determinant of life chances. Equality requires democracy, the process through which we meet as equals and negotiate our collective dilemmas.

To this end we need to develop a culture and politics of respect and recognition throughout civil society. Such a culture is guided by mutuality and reciprocity. Its democratic ethos contests the current values of competition, individual acquisition and self interest, which legitimise inequality and the unfair distribution of life chances. To be denied recognition because of our class, sexuality, gender, colour, religion or disability – and so be considered different from the 'norm' – is to experience not just inferiority but invisibility. It is a form of social humiliation and shaming, often destroying self esteem. A society that makes large numbers of its citizens feel they are looked down on will inevitably incur the costs of people's antisocial reactions to the structures that demean them.

Redistribution means addressing wealth as well as poverty, for instance by framing taxation policy as an expression of the citizenship obligations of the better off (instead of focusing always on the obligations of benefit recipients). Taxation in the UK is presently not progressive – the poorest pay a larger share of their income in tax than others. We must move towards a fair and progressive tax system. This is further detailed in A New Political Economy. We believe that wages and benefits should be high enough to be compatible with human dignity. In chapter five we advocate a living wage. These measures need to be accompanied by a widespread debate about the overall distribution of pay, and the rewards attached to different kinds of work. The inequality gap should not be so large as to prevent recognition, or to fracture the bonds of common citizenship.

Policies aimed at reducing levels of inequality are often developed in isolation from one another. Social investment must be aimed at the causes of inequality, not the symptoms. By investing in solutions to the causes of crime, violence, poverty, ill health, stress and discrimination, the Treasury will save billions in the longer term. For example it is increasingly recognised that investment in the early years of a child's life can reduce later inequalities and pay itself back many times through health and educational outcomes and reduced social disruption.

All this requires a holistic and 'joined up' approach to formulating policies, and a method for evaluating their impact on reducing inequality. That is why we support the Fabian Commission on Life Chances argument that all policies, including public service reform, should be judged against the 'litmus test' of their impact on life chances. This would identify policies that would have a detrimental effect on life chances and prevent them from being enacted, and promote policy-making that would improve the life chances of the worst off. This kind of approach would put inequality at the heart of all policy-making and would help us move towards a society where everybody has access to the resources they need to live a good life.

3 Making UK poverty history

Under successive Conservative governments poverty rose remorselessly. Between 1979 and 1996 the number of households without any assets doubled to 1 in 10. New Labour has sought to decrease poverty, and it is now 2 million below its peak of the mid-1990s. Poverty levels are still very high however: more than 11 million people in Britain, including more than 3 million children, still live in poverty.

It has been a significant achievement of the New Labour government that the eradication of child poverty is now a public policy goal shared by all the main political parties. However, while a significant reduction of 700,000 has been achieved, the government has missed the first target it set itself, and the future targets will be even harder to achieve, since they require lifting out of poverty the most excluded groups, who are the hardest to reach. Poverty will never become history through a strategy based on mechanical cash transfers that are not based on widespread public support. Redistribution by stealth is hitting a roadblock.

We need to confront the cultural legacy of the past in which poverty was viewed as a personal failing. Individuals living in poverty and forced to exist on state benefits suffer shame because society mirrors back to them demeaning and contemptible definitions of themselves. The term the 'underclass' is stigmatising. The mantra of 'hard-working families' contains the unspoken judgement on those who are deemed to be losers, recreating historically rooted divisions between 'deserving' and 'undeserving' poor. Stigmatising language is not only harmful to those it describes. By making those in poverty different from the rest of society, it separates 'them' from 'us', reinforcing the anxiety, contempt and divisions created by inequality. Comfortable Britain is more likely to write 'the poor' off as beyond the bonds of common citizenship than to respond to appeals based on enlightened self-interest to support a concerted attack on poverty.

Poverty is about lack of money, inadequate living standards, feeling powerless to change the situation and being looked down upon. The result is a grinding and exhausting struggle to maintain body and soul. We need a systematic and long-term approach to its eradication; a new kind of politics which is about the moral principle of the equal worth of each individual. To this end the primary goal is a more equal distribution of both disposable (post tax-benefit) and original income, and of wealth. We need to increase the incomes and assets of those living in poverty through benefits and wages if they are to live flourishing lives.

Government today claims that the best route out of poverty is work. A full-time wage markedly reduces the risk of poverty. But paid work alone is no panacea. Half of the children in poverty in Britain today live in households where someone works but is on a low wage. And work is not always appropriate or possible, because of caring responsibilities or severe health problems. Furthermore, not all who want paid work can find it, due to lack of appropriate jobs or because of barriers to the labour market.

While New Labour has managed to improve the lives of a proportion of children living in poverty, adult benefit rates have stagnated. There are now an increasing number of working-age, childless adults living in poverty. The single adult rate of Income Support declined as a proportion of average earnings from 13.4 per cent in April 1997 to 11.0 per cent in April 2004. The couple rate declined from 21 to 17.3 per cent. The dismal inadequacy of these rates affects not only childless adults but also parents and parents-to-be. They have knock-on effects on their children, however hard they work to protect them against the full impact of poverty. Mothers bear the main strain of managing poverty.

Young mothers receive an even lower benefit rate than adults and mothers-to-be.[11] A poverty income during pregnancy makes it harder for women to eat well and this can impact on the future health of their babies. The infant mortality rate among the children of those living in poverty is double that for children born to the middle classes.

Policy strategies for renewal

We need to deal simultaneously with the causes and symptoms of poverty. Some of the causes are to do with the nature of our economic system, and these are explored in A New Political Economy. Policy strategies to tackle poverty need to be reintegrated into the wider discussion about quality of life. Dealing with poverty is one crucial part of a wider story about building a good society in which we all have access to the things we need to flourish. Integral to this is the environmental agenda. People living in poverty invariably live in the worst local environments. More generally, some environmental measures can have a regressive impact. Care must be taken to build any sustainable development agenda hand in hand with a social justice agenda.

New Labour has kept silent about the positive steps it has taken to address poverty. Perhaps this has been through fear of how the electorate would respond to redistribution. The Fabian Society Commission on Life Chances research provides evidence that when people are made aware of the scale of the poverty problem, and are shown how government action can make a difference, they respond positively. In fact they are willing to countenance higher taxation to pay for dealing with child poverty. Mass support can be mobilised to create a society in which everybody can flourish.

Social justice is not just about outcomes, it is about dignity. The culture of respect and recognition needs to be extended into the formulation and delivery of anti-poverty policies. People with experience of poverty must have a voice and influence in decision-making. Professionals and officials need training in poverty-awareness. As one person living in poverty describes it: 'it is about how we are treated, we just want them to treat us the same way they want us to treat them – with respect'.

Poverty is not a singular experience. It impacts on some specific groups more than others. For example, the poverty rate amongst children of Pakistani and Bangladeshi origin is 61 per cent. And the one in five people in rural areas living in poverty tend to get overlooked. Tackling rural poverty requires different approaches which research needs to address. And whilst the proportion of pensioners in poverty has fallen from 27 per cent in 1995 to 17 per cent in 2005, we need a sustainable pensions system, as we explore in chapter 8.

Research shows that the government could meet its target of halving child poverty by 2010 through spending £4 billion (0.3 per cent of GDP) more than is currently planned on taxes and benefits – not a great deal in the scheme of things.[12] This could be done through raising the child element of Child Tax Credit to £48.50 from £37, and the family element by £20 each for third and subsequent children. To get the other half of children out of poverty by 2020 will be harder. It will need a combination of increases in benefits and tax credits and a range of other measures to help disadvantaged groups, such as improving educational outcomes and targeting public services towards the worst off.

Increases in children's benefits have contributed to the decrease in child poverty. However, apart from a one-off real rise in child benefit for the first child during the government's first term, it has been means-tested support for children that has been increased, and this has brought with it all the usual problems associated with means-testing, such as low take up and the creation of a poverty trap. The time has come for a further real increase in the universal child benefit, especially for second and subsequent children.

It is not just children who suffer from poverty. Current benefit levels in general are too low to provide for a dignified standard of living. More adequate benefit levels could be set through an independent Minimum Income Standards Commission, whose impartiality could create a public consensus to benchmark required benefit levels annually against living costs. With these measures, alongside our tax proposals in *A New Political Economy*, and the proposals suggested later in this book for a living wage, Participation Income and care policies, we can start with confidence to make poverty in the UK history.

4 Crime and punishment

Crime undermines our confidence in society. To be mugged or threatened on the street or to have one's home burgled is to experience a fundamental attack on one's sense of self. Alongside the loss of one's possessions, the feelings of humiliation, shame and dread can destroy self-confidence.

Worse still is the blight of violence in our society. Not just the public fights and pub brawls, but racist assaults, insidious bullying at work and school, homophobic attacks, and the high levels of domestic violence mainly inflicted by men on their wives and partners. To be assaulted, or to live in fear of violence, is a violation of one's integrity and worth as an individual human being. In our insecure society, fear of crime reflects this pervasive anxiety of being violated, not just physically but psychologically. This is why the tabloid press, with its agenda of retribution and punishment, can sustain high levels of public anxiety at a time of falling crime rates. Crime is a major social problem and our goal must be to reduce it. But to do this will involve challenging prejudices that are promoted by tabloid justice.

Alcohol-fuelled violence, persistent petty offending, theft to finance drug habits, and criminal behaviour aggravated by mental illness are some of the acute social problems that intensify our insecurity and fear of crime. In this climate, and aided by scare stories in the media, prison comes to be seen as the bastion of law and order that will deter crime, promote social peace and satisfy a desire for retribution.

But in reality our prison system does not achieve this. It is the sink into which we pour the human damage and social problems created by inequality and poverty, so as to temporarily rid ourselves of them. More than half the crime in Britain is committed by people who have already been through the criminal justice system. As the prison population has risen to its current record level of nearly 78,000, so too have reconviction rates. In 1992, 51 per cent of those leaving prison were reconvicted. By 2004 the proportion had risen to 67 per cent, and for young men aged 18 to 21 the proportion is a staggering 78.4

per cent. The annual cost of a prison place is £40,992, and a conservative estimate of the annual cost of re-offending is £11 billion.[13] The more we imprison, the less effective prison is in deterring crime and the more expensive it becomes.

England and Wales now has the highest imprisonment rate in Western Europe. And yet the 2003 Criminal Justice Act provides the capacity to vastly increase the rate of imprisonment in the future. When the prison system once again bursts at the seams with overcrowding, where shall we incarcerate the ever-increasing flow of prisoners – floating hulks, offshore islands, oil rigs, army camps? The crisis of our prison system reveals a society that doesn't know what to do with the social problems it has created.

Who are the increasing numbers of people that we are locking up? These are not career criminals. Their collective profile provides a shameful insight into the injustices and inequalities of the last three decades. Their average age is 27, with a quarter under 22. 27 per cent were taken into care as children (compared to 2 per cent of the general population); 52 per cent of male convicts and 71 per cent of female convicts have no qualifications; 65 per cent are innumerate and 48 per cent illiterate. Before entering prison, 67 per cent were unemployed and 32 per cent were homeless. The growth of punishment and New Labour's 'tough' approach to crime has been at the expense of the most vulnerable. The number of women, children and the elderly imprisoned has risen at a substantially higher rate than the average increase. For those who experience the imprisonment of their mother, the outlook is particularly bleak; only 5 per cent remain in their own home. Imprisonment does not lead to a more secure society. It mirrors the social injustices of inequality, and impacts most severely on deprived communities.[14]

The startling growth in the prison population is not a consequence of an increase in crime. It is not a result of finding and catching more criminals. The courts are not prosecuting more people accused of committing serious crimes. The number found guilty of more serious offences has remained largely constant over recent years.

The key explanation for the rising numbers in prison is the increased severity in sentencing. In 1991, 15 per cent of those found guilty of an indictable offence received a custodial sentence. By 2001 it had increased to 25 per cent. The harsher levels of sentencing can be seen clearly when considering individual offence types. For example, a first time domestic burglar had a 27 per cent chance of receiving a custodial sentence in 1995/96. By 2000 this had increased to 48 per cent. At the same time, the average sentence length had increased from 16 to 18 months.

The essential point is that we are not undergoing a crime wave, but a punishment wave. And if sentences are growing now, at a time of falling crime, imagine the kind of increase we will face during an economic recession.

We cannot build a tolerant society on the basis of zero tolerance.

Policy strategies for renewal

The make up of the prison population, often generations of one family in the same prison, is an indicator of the effects of poverty and inequality on society, and a measure of the failures of our public service provision. This is not to seek to justify the perpetrators of crime, but we cannot separate criminal justice from social justice.

Crime flourishes in areas of deprivation, and disproportionately affects those living in poverty. Only by addressing the causes of crime will we end the permanent growth of the prison system. Fifteen years of prison building has demonstrably failed to bring any kind of social peace or serenity. Tackling the social recession will involve reforming the criminal justice system and reducing the prison population. We can start by addressing three factors: mental health, drugs and alcohol.

Many people suffering from mental illness are swept out of sight into prisons. 72 per cent of men in prison suffer two or more mental disorders, compared with 5 per cent in the general population. Thousands are so seriously mentally ill that they require immediate transfer to the NHS. Prison is itself a significant cause of mental ill health. Half of women in prison harm themselves, while the suicide rate for men in prison is five times higher than in the general population – and eighteen times higher for boys aged 15 to 17. The lack of places of safety in the community, at all levels of security, is a major factor in the increasing use of prison to contain the mentally ill.

Most acquisitive crime is fuelled by drugs. Over half of prisoners report committing offences connected to their drug taking. Officers at HMP Manchester estimated that 70 per cent of prisoners had a drug problem, and of these 80 per cent had never had any contact with drug treatment services. Drug use goes hand in hand with the kind of chaotic behaviour that causes people to miss court hearings, community punishments, and probation appointments. As a result they get sent to, or recalled to, prison for comparatively petty offences. Because the tendency is to view drug abuse as a criminal matter or a moral failing, it becomes a problem for the criminal justice system to manage. People who are addicted end up being punished rather than treated. This approach dismally fails to alleviate the problem, and it is dangerous to the health of addicts. It is the easy option, but the expensive one – a prison place is more expensive than residential drug treatment.

Most violent crime and public disorder offences are driven by alcohol. Around three-fifths of male sentenced prisoners and two-fifths of females admit to levels of drinking that are hazardous to their mental and physical health. In the latest British Crime Survey, almost half of victims of violent crime report that the perpetrator was under the influence of alcohol. Over half of alcohol-related violence occurs in and around pubs, clubs and discos, mostly at the weekend. Alcohol also causes death and casualties through road accidents, and is a significant contributory factor in injury and victimisation, domestic violence and sexual assault.

Locking up drug addicts and hazardous drinkers almost never breaks the grip of a serious addiction and almost always submerges people further in the world of criminality. Prison should be for those who pose a danger to the public, a place where time is used constructively to reduce the risk of re-offending, with the aim of protecting future potential victims of crime. We need to stop using prisons as a dumping ground for the mentally ill, and those with drug and alcohol addictions.

The vast majority of women sent to prison have not committed serious or violent crimes. Two thirds are on remand, very many for psychiatric assessment. Most of these women are also mothers. They need community-based support and supervision – help with drugs, drinking, mental healthcare and debt recovery – which can break the pattern of offending without destroying families. Locking up vulnerable children is the quickest way to create the criminals of the future. Re-offending rates soar to over 80 per cent for this age group. They need secure care, specialist fostering, intensive supervision and mentoring.

To tackle crime and create a secure society involves 'justice reinvestment' in real social change – investment to create a society of equal life chances.

Justice reinvestment means redefining ideas of public safety, and investing prison money in measures to alleviate the social causes of crime. The money could be used to fund services, and, for example, job creation and training in low-income neighbourhoods. Or it could help fund Primary Care Trusts, who must be required to fulfil their responsibility to provide court diversion schemes for the mentally ill. Additional investment can be made in medium secure healthcare places and halfway houses. Justice reinvestment can make a major impact on reducing drug and alcohol fuelled crime. We need to develop treatment programmes to rehabilitate people with drug and alcohol addictions. Our goal is to reduce the numbers of victims of crime and to create a secure society. To achieve this goal we must significantly cut the numbers of people we lock up and begin treating the causes not the symptoms of crime.

5 Time poor and overworked

The feeling of being useful, able to employ our knowledge, experience and skills to a good end, is a major source of well-being. Work connects us to a community. It is a valuable source of self-esteem. Today there are more varied, enriching and stimulating kinds of work than ever before – but only for a minority of people. The pleasures to be gained in work and the opportunities for creative labour have been greatly reduced in the last few decades. The economy is shaped like an hourglass, with those at the top doing relatively well and those at the bottom struggling to get by. The narrow funnel between the two defines the limits of social justice.

Rising levels of inequality have been accompanied by an intensification of work and a culture of time poverty. British men are working the longest hours in Europe. Women's (especially mothers') participation in the labour market has increased. During the 1990s job satisfaction fell sharply. Between 40 and 60 per cent of the entire labour force found their workloads increasing and their hours getting longer. In the average UK household (where at least one adult is employed), the amount of time spent in paid work in a year increased by 7.6 weeks between 1998 and 1981.[15]

Work related stress has become a major source of ill health.[16] Employees in their thirties are the most discontented and experience the most stress, as they juggle long working hours and family life.[17] This overwork culture has prompted virtually no public protest just lone despair. One cause has been the diminished influence of trade unions, undermined by anti-union legislation, and suffering a substantial loss in membership in the 1990s.

Large numbers of workers earn relatively low wages in mundane jobs. The wages of factory workers, teachers and university lecturers have all declined relative to the average.[18] Training tends to go to those already most qualified, and there are often few incentives for companies to provide staff development.

Market-based reform in the public sector has introduced a managerial culture of audit targets, tests, quality assurance and performance indicators. Professional self-discipline and trust has been replaced by a form of social surveillance in which individuals are constantly called to account, creating a high degree of uncertainty and a fear of being constantly judged. This continuous process of auditing and monitoring has marginalised the old ethos of public service, and there has been a startling demoralisation amongst public sector professionals. A survey by the qualifications authority City and Guilds reported that only 17 per cent of health professionals, 8 per cent of teachers and 2 per cent of social workers said they were happy with their jobs.

Amongst the low-paid, the problems are poverty and exploitation, insecurity, and a lack of control over one's work. The short-term contracts and casualised labour of the flexible employment market have shifted the burden of risk – costs of education, training, ill health, being made redundant – from business and the state to the individual. The less well paid a worker, the harsher the risks they face.

But the economic security of the middle classes has also diminished, as white-collar jobs are threatened by global outsourcing. The flattened, networked structure of companies that have outsourced and casualised parts of their labour force have made obsolete traditional career progression. The old style corporate management of employees has given way to control through performance-related pay and targets, in which trust, commitment and loyalty are all diminished. Constant change throws into doubt the task and ethos of organisations, disrupting the roles and identities of their workers. Employees increasingly become their own timekeepers, taking work home, blurring the divide between work, home and personal life.

For a large group of people there is a growing concern about becoming useless, because of competition from a better educated and cheaper global workforce, technological innovation, or the obsolescence of their skills and training. While the new culture of work has enhanced the working lives of a small minority of 'creative' workers in the knowledge and cultural industries, the benefits have not been extended to the majority. For most of us it has meant increasing levels of anxiety about an unforeseeable and unpredictable future.

The demands for increased efficiency, the increases in time at work and the extending of job responsibilities have brought stress and anxiety to millions. Yet the productivity of the British economy still lags behind that of France and

Germany.

The new culture of work has reduced the time available for family life and the pursuit of personal interests. We are subject to a time-economy imposed by the quest for profit, and it is having a serious impact on our well-being. There is considerable evidence that Britain's record on 'work-life' balance is the worst in the EU. British men and women are the most likely to express a desire for a reduction in working hours in order to spend more time with their families. But part-time workers, most of whom are women, are the most disadvantaged in terms of pay, tenure and employment protection. Society is in the grip of a 'time famine'. We are constantly rushed and harried, in a long hours, high spending culture.

Nevertheless, people are seeking to shift their behaviour within the constraints they face. A study by Cambridge University in 2003 found that, despite increasing pressures to earn and spend more, over a quarter of British adults aged 30-59 voluntarily made a long-term change in lifestyle in the past decade that resulted in earning less money. And downshifting is not confined to wealthy middle-aged people. It is spread fairly evenly across age groups and social grades, with only a slightly higher proportion from social grades A and B. The most common reason given for making this change is the desire to spend more time with family, especially amongst people in their 30s and 40s. People hunger for more meaningful time rather than simple material success.

Access to meaningful, disposable time can be seen as a primary good in itself and as a means to other – economic, social, political and personal – ends. Its distribution is a matter of social justice. Some groups have more access than others to time that they can spend as they wish. The 'usefulness' of disposable time is not simply a matter of total hours free of other commitments. It varies according to a number of factors: whether it is fragmented or in a block, whether or not it is supported by other resources, and its predictability. As is argued in the third Compass Programme for Renewal book, *Democracy and the Public Realm,* civil society depends upon our having time to give to it: we can only engage in voluntary work or participate fully in democracy if we have the time to do so.

There is an unequal distribution of working, caring and disposable time between and within households. Continuing inequalities in the home advantage men in the workplace and politics. Despite women now spending a lot more time in the workplace and men contributing somewhat more in the home, the domestic division of labour remains highly unequal. The problem is men's 'domestic absenteeism', their unwillingness or inability to contribute more at home. The market-driven solution has been to shift formerly unpaid domestic and caring work to paid workers, either individually employed as part of a new servant class, or in nurseries and care homes. This kind of emotional labour is usually badly paid, and it is often undertaken by migrants, thereby displacing the 'care deficit' to their own families.

In the good society we would have the right both to give and to receive care without being financially punished. Such a society would value and reward time spent on caring for others as much as time spent on other socially important activities – supporting women's traditional responsibilities while opening them up to men.

The good society promotes an ethic of care, not the work ethic.

Policy strategies for renewal

Despite the time famine there is little discussion about how we might improve working life. Democratic trade unions remain essential for the defence of worker's interests (the issue of trade unions is addressed in *Democracy and the Public Realm*). But we also need to create new forms of economic citizenship, and to bring the economy and work under greater democratic control. Other ideas around the quality of working life are put forward in *A New Political Economy*.

One important aspect of healthy workplaces is the amount of control people have over their work and the quality of their social relations. We need to create institutional cultures at work that promote participation and trust. For example, quality circles can create forums to identify grievances, provide mutual support and develop innovative ideas. They suggest more open and democratic organisations in which management is more accountable, and is based on trust and communication.

Greater democracy at work can also be developed through employee owned and controlled companies. This not only accords with social justice; it could also offer major economic and social advantages. Companies combining partial employee share ownership schemes with 'participative' management methods experience significant improvements in productivity. John Lewis Partnership is an example of such a company. Employee ownership can change the idea of business: instead of being seen as a piece of property it could be seen as a working community.

An immediate priority should be the workers at the bottom of the labour market who experience the poorest conditions.[19] Often they are migrants in extremely low paid work as cleaners, security guards, carers. They are frequently employed by agencies, allowing the organisation using their services to deny them the same terms and conditions they give their own employees.

More than a quarter of all low paid workers are employed within education, health and local and central government. Increasing their pay and improving their conditions would have a major impact on low paid work in the UK. It would contribute to forcing private sector employers who are competing for the same workers to improve wages. It would also make a major contribution to narrowing the gender pay gap.

In East London, the community organisation London Citizens initiated a campaign for a living wage amongst office cleaners in the City. The success and growing impact of the Living Wage Campaign as it takes on the big banks, universities and the 2012 Olympics is proof that successful mass campaigning is alive and well.

Too many people in this country struggle to survive on exploitative levels of low pay. The current minimum wage is now below what people need to lead a dignified life. It should be improved towards a 'living wage'. The Greater London Authority has calculated a figure for London in 2006 of £7.05 an hour. This would enable a worker to make ends meet for themselves and their family. Why should companies get away with paying less than it costs to live?

A standard living wage should be introduced across the country. This should be part of a 'New Deal on Low Pay'. The public sector should improve pay and conditions for low paid workers. They can do this through their own employment conditions and also through their buying power by insisting on certain minimum conditions for any staff they employ through agencies.

Time, like wealth and income, is a basic good that we all need to lead a good life. Meaningful time is an indicator of quality of life and the health of a democracy. A politics of time will have far reaching consequences. We need to improve the balance between work and family life, improving family leave provision for men as well as women. This would also cover time to care for family members other than children. Employment policies need to assume that 'normal' workers have family responsibilities, that they are civically active and that they have non-work interests. The current rhetoric around 'family-friendly' policies and 'work-life' balance needs to be taken seriously to rid Britain of its long-hours culture. One step towards this would be full implementation of the EU Working Time Directive and an end to the 'opt out' which perpetuates the long hours culture.

The just distribution of time presupposes the just distribution of incomes and wealth. To do this we must accommodate non-waged, care and other socially valuable activities by uncoupling work from paid employment.

The social security system could be reformed so that the distinction between being in work and being out of work becomes less fixed, and activities such as caring or volunteering are recognised as contributions to society which require support. One example of such a reform is the Netherlands scheme whereby parents of young children can work 75 per cent of their normal hours and receive a parental benefit for the remaining 25 per cent, in order to encourage shared parental care and domestic work. In contrast Britain confines itself to a childcare element to the Working Tax credit, which can cover 80 per cent of the costs of child care for a single child, at a rate of up to £175 per week. In the shorter term the right to pay relatives and or close friends for care could be extended through the Working Tax Credit system, and through Direct Payments given to older people and disabled people with care needs.

At the same time, a Participation Income scheme can be piloted with a view to introducing it in the medium term. A Participation Income is an income for those that are active in employment, volunteering, learning or caring (as well as children, the elderly, people who are ill and people with disabilities). It recognises that there is value in activity beyond paid employment and therefore validates other ways of spending our time. In the longer term, and in a society where we have succeeded in eradicating systemic poverty, and where wealth and income inequalities have been sufficiently reduced, a public debate can be initiated around the idea of extending the Participation Income into the universal entitlement of a Citizen's Income – a basic unconditional income for all.

6 From the work ethic to an ethic of care

Who cares for those in need? The concept of 'care' refers to a number of types of relationships, in which there is a presumption both of 'caring for' and 'caring about' others. The giving and receiving of care and support takes place in relationships where people are unable to care entirely for themselves because they are very young, very old, frail or disabled.

Like time, care is an issue of social justice. The relative powerlessness associated with the dependency of children and older people and some disabled people makes them vulnerable to abuse and lack of 'voice'. Because of their lack of access to the labour market the vulnerable are impoverished. The assumption that caring is women's responsibility results in gender inequalities: caring impedes access to the labour market, which reduces the earning power of those who care – usually women. Unpaid care work is often invisible, despite contributing significantly to society and the economy. Those in paid care work – also mostly women – are low paid. The more unequal and polarised a society, the more people on low incomes provide for the care needs of the better off.

The public provision of care – childcare, elder care – is necessarily expensive. It has no intrinsic productivity. You can increase the number of people carers care for, but only by sacrificing quality. If the market provides care, its cost rises as wages rise. This means that care workers' wages are always being forced down, and good quality care is always jeopardised. Avoiding this requires public subsidies for care. However, not all care work can be institutionalised – nor do people want this. They want to be able to participate in the public sphere and spend time with each other and their children.

Developing political strategies around care needs to take into account the social changes of recent decades. Women's increased participation in the workforce has made redundant the old assumptions that they will provide the unpaid labour of care. At the same time, the ageing population is increasing the need for care. The Wanless Social Care Review reports that the numbers of older people with both high and low levels of need are set to increase by over 50 per cent in the next decade.[20] Children are financially dependent on their parents for longer. There is less experience of life-long marriage or life-long work. A multi-cultural and global society makes for a diversity of family traditions as well as care commitments, which are stretched across continents. There is a growing acknowledgment of same-sex relationships, and that friends constitute an important source of care and support.

More public support is needed for care. But the government too easily ignores the quality of care in seeking cheap solutions using a poorly regulated private sector, and supporting families through tax credits to buy their own care. What matters is the quality of care while maintaining respect and dignity. Good quality care minimises stress, creates emotionally stable people, and overall has the potential to improve social solidarity and well-being. This in itself is a valuable investment in the future.

An ethic of care is rooted in an assumption of people's interdependence, unlike the work ethic that assumes individuals are free of need and entirely self sufficient. To give and receive care in conditions of mutual respect is in and of itself part of being a citizen, because one acquires the skills of being respectful, of being attentive to and mindful of the frailty of others. These are not only personal dispositions, they are also civic virtues.[21]

Policy strategies for renewal

To achieve a more 'caring' society of the future, a wide range of policies would need to be introduced to underpin a new public service ethos. At the centre of this new ethic and practice of care would be the acknowledgment of interdependence and support for human dignity, flourishing and mutual respect. A new public service ethos would be informed by responsiveness and responsibility. It would ensure care workers receive a 'living wage'.

Care and the relationships in which it is embedded are central to the meaning and purpose of people's lives. Providing it with recognition and value through an ethic of care has widespread implications for the organisation of work, social security, housing, health and welfare services, education and family law.

In the long term, we need to create a national infrastructure of the care economy – a new kind of welfare state for the twenty-first century, which invests in the emotional and psychological well-being of citizens, particularly children. We could build on the Sure Start schemes, embedding them in local communities, entrusting them more to the participants and workers, and ensuring that they do not become top-down forms of social engineering. Current proposals for Children's Centres could be extended and increased to provide a network of neighbourhood centres, offering a range of care services: nursery care, playgroups, day care, and home care services such as cleaning, laundry, and cheap healthy food. Other services could include legal advice, free therapeutic help and relationship support. The longer term social dividends and financial savings from such an investment would be enormous.

We can begin this long-term process by developing a high quality system of childcare. Recent work in neuroscience has confirmed that the emotional development of children starts from the moment of their birth. The most intense period of socialisation occurs in the first two years of life. The way that psychological needs are met in infancy and early childhood plays a major role in determining the kinds of adults and citizens children become.

Society requires a modern public service of childcare, centred on the emotional development of children, and working to reduce child poverty, help strengthen family relationships and parenting, and enable a better balance between work and life. Childcare should not be attempted on the cheap, nor should it be organised to meet the demands of today's working patterns. Working patterns need to change in order to fit in with the needs of children.

Fundamental to the development of a high quality childcare service is the need to invest heavily in its workforce. We need to create a self-confident profession, with its own career structure and signed up to the new public service ethos. At present childcare workers are under-qualified and earn, on average, less than supermarket workers (the average salary is £7,500 compared to £22,000 for a primary school teacher). Few are likely to be tempted into training for higher qualifications for such meagre rewards. We need to address these workforce issues. There should be parity of esteem and pay with school teachers.

To ensure the quality and the well-being of children, childcare services will need to be publicly funded. We can take as a model the advanced childcare systems and pedagogic values of the Nordic countries, which now have a universal entitlement to childcare for all children from at least 12 months of age, regardless of parental employment status. Provision is underpinned by good opportunities for parental leave, a well-trained workforce, sustained investment in services, and a well-developed sense of the value of childcare to children. These services are heavily subsidised and parental fees account for just a small proportion of the total costs (11 per cent in Sweden, and 33 per cent in Denmark, for example). This has only been possible because the Nordic countries have invested at least six times the proportion of spending that the UK allocates for childcare.

There is also a need for a far stronger social care system in the UK. The Wanless review reported that there are half a million adults in the UK whose social care needs are not being met. There is popular support to improve the system. 50 per cent of respondents to a MORI poll backed paying higher taxes for improved social care, as against 26 per cent who opposed it. Our model of social care is out of date. There is a duty on local authorities to provide certain limited services, but individuals have no rights to receive support, and in particular no right to refuse to live in a residential home. We need a social care system designed to help people lead the kinds of lives that they would like. Social care must be about ensuring a dignified life and the same substantive freedoms as others in society. Scotland has made a start by introducing free social care. This could be extended across the rest of the UK. Lord Ashley's private member's bill on 'Independent Living' provides an indication of the kind of system that is required – user-centred, and focused on creating independence rather than dependence. Investing in social care now is an investment in all our futures.

7 Coming of age – children's lives today

Childhood, the saying goes, should be the best years of one's life. And today children are provided for in a way that would have been unimaginable even fifty years ago. Television channels cater for their interests. There are fashion outlets exclusive to children. A pop industry revolves around their tastes in music and teen idols. Comics, films and magazines and a rich contemporary literature enhance their cultural worlds. School activities, educational visits and exchanges and the growth in overseas holidays have provided many with knowledge of other people and places. In social life the growth of games technologies has opened up new avenues of leisure and education. My-Space, Facebook, Friendster and bebo provide the young with new opportunities for creating online social worlds and networks. And the old generational distance between parents and their children seems to have shrunk; the trend is towards more democratic families, where children are listened to and their opinions respected. We live in a culture of prosperity and opportunity that should be enriching children's lives.

And yet in recent years growing numbers of children are failing to flourish. They are targeted as consumers with promises of the fulfilment of their wishes, but they remain relatively powerless and poorly served as citizens with rights. Children and young people have been hit hard by the social recession of the past three decades.

While the government has succeeded in reducing child poverty, it remains an indictment of our society. Poverty and poor diet have led to a serious increase in obesity amongst children.[22] A generation is at risk of type 2 diabetes, cardiovascular diseases and premature death. The Nuffield Foundation has identified a sharp decline in the mental health of teenagers. Behavioural problems amongst adolescents have more than doubled over the last twenty-five years, whilst emotional problems such as depression, anxiety and hyperactivity have increased by 70 per cent.[23] Research conducted by the University of Oxford's Centre for Suicide Research found that 10 per cent of 15 and 16 year olds have deliberately self-harmed, the majority (64 per cent) by cutting themselves.[24] Dr Andrew McCulloch of the Mental Health Foundation has described, a 'shocking decline in the mental health of our teenagers. The epidemic of self-harm among young people in the UK may only be a precursor to a mental-health crisis among this generation'.[25]

As a society we have to face up to some of the negative ways we treat children. A decade ago a large-scale government-commissioned research study, interviewing parents and children, found very high rates of corporal punishment in the home, including severe punishment.[26] 91 per cent of children had been hit. In families where both parents were interviewed, it was found that almost half the children were hit weekly or more often; 35 per cent had been punished 'severely'. 'Severe' punishments were those 'that were intended to, had the potential to, or actually did cause harm to the child, and included actions that were repeated, prolonged, or involved the use of implements'. Since then, attitudes toward hitting children are changing and there are now 170 MPs who support granting them the same legal protection from assault as adults. Children have a right not to be hit. Many children attempt to deal with problems at home by running away. The Children's Society put the figure at 100,000 under sixteen year olds each year: 25 per cent of these are under the age of 11.

Outside of the home, it can be argued that very little education currently takes place in our schools. The need to pass tests has meant a huge focus on the appearance of education rather than its reality. Ten-year-olds are drilled for a year or more to get through exams at eleven, only for their secondary schools to retest them and discover that they cannot actually work at that level. They have learnt tricks and techniques, but not understanding. Ofsted now reports that very few sixteen year olds can write essays unaided. The priority to get them through the coursework and the exams at the highest level possible means that schools cannot risk children doing their own thinking.

Everybody loses. Children living in poverty and hard-pressed areas fall further behind with every passing year. Some children are utterly dispirited by trudging over the same ground. Every child learns that their input, their interests, their responses are not wanted. It's no surprise that we end up with high levels of truancy, disruption, adolescent ill health and sadness. No-one is happy with the end products. Employers and universities alike say the quality of school-leavers is falling and that they are lacking in the skills of teamworking, problem-solving, creativity and the ability to learn independently. If children have any of these talents at the end of their years in the system, it's a tribute to exceptional teachers or the resilience of the children's spirit.

In recent years increasing numbers of working-class children have been demonised as 'feral children'. The resulting anti-social behaviour legislation relies on a low burden of proof and blurs the boundaries between civil and criminal law, with serious implications for due process and the rights of the child. Involvement in activities that merit a civic sanction can lead to the imprisonment of children who breach an anti-social behaviour order (ASBO). The policy of naming and the consequent shaming of children is retributive and counter productive. ASBOs and custodial treatment for children under 16 should be replaced with intensive support for persistent perpetrators and their parents.

Policy strategies for renewal

The state needs to take a lead in recovering the mental and physical well-being of all children and ensuring that collective provision exists for their care and development from the beginning of life. As we set out in the section on poverty, we need to start tackling childhood deprivation by ending adult poverty and focusing resources on parents to be, particularly mothers, and, as set out in the section on care, we need a universal system of childcare.

Children's well-being is closely related to the question of their citizenship, particularly their social and economic rights (even if children enjoy some of these rights by proxy). We need to make sure that human rights are fully extended to children. Their active participation in society not only safeguards their well-being in the present, it also enables them to develop their capacities for self-fulfilment and to become skilled citizens of the future. At the same time, there needs to be greater recognition of the extent to which children are already exercising responsibilities of citizenship – as workers, carers and participants in civic life.

Children are subjected to very powerful marketing forces, which impact upon their desires and their values. By the age of ten the average British child can recognise nearly 400 brand names. Almost 70 per cent of three year olds recognise the McDonald's symbol, but less than half of them know their own surname. Research has found that children's exposure to the media predicts higher consumer involvement. Consumer involvement in turn predicts higher rates of depression, anxiety, and psychosomatic complaints such as headaches and boredom, as well as lower self-esteem. The targeting of children by companies is now a major concern to the great majority of parents. Children need to be protected from the full force of marketisation until they are able to understand that they are being marketed to. We need to restrict advertising aimed at children. A change in legislation to make advertising to children unlawful could follow the example of Sweden's 1995 Marketing Act, which bans commercials designed to attract the attention of children under the age of 12.

If we are to develop a more egalitarian and democratic approach to childhood and child development, we need to continue with reforms to education and the culture of schooling. New Labour has made education one of its central priorities. It has invested large sums in improving existing buildings, training headteachers, increasing the numbers of teachers and classroom assistants, reducing class sizes and building new schools. But its commitment to improving the life chances of children has been rooted in an approach to education that is controlling, instrumental and test-driven. Education is reduced to a means of preparing young people for the jobs market and improving national competitiveness. It is an approach to the learning process in which play, the imagination and creativity play little part.

Despite its good intentions and improvements in educational standards, the current system of schooling stifles children's natural propensity to learn about life and to become well rounded human beings. It also continues to favour middle-class children, promoting their advantage through the accumulation of credentials that open the door to the next rung of the educational ladder, and privileged access in the labour market. Schools are the gatekeepers of the labour market and as such they can serve to reproduce class inequalities and social injustice.

We would recommend replacing the current testing and target-centred culture for one which supports children in developing their emotional, physical, intellectual and creative capabilities – education in which play, imagination and relationships take more prominent roles. In England pupils are tested at the ages of 7, 11, 14, 16, 17 and 18, creating a treadmill of stress and anxiety throughout childhood.

There are two key questions for the transformation of the culture of schooling. Are all of our children getting the resources and skills they will need in order to develop their capacities for a flourishing life? How can we impart these to them in a way that will make them feel like valued members of society while they are going through the process? There is no single policy that will create an education for flourishing. Rather we need to initiate a cultural transformation of our education system over the next decade, so that it becomes one that enables children to flourish and to meet the demands of today's society.

Some of this approach has been adopted in Wales where the new education policy will abolish Key-Stage 1 (testing has already been ended) and bring together early years schooling and pre-schooling to create a Foundation Stage for the 3-7 age range. Children's play is given its rightful place: 'children spend too much time doing tasks while sitting at tables rather than learning through well-designed opportunities for play . . . For young children – when they play – it is their work'.[26]

For children, learning is about play, creativity, and the imagination. In later childhood, it is the opportunity to discover the capacity to think for one's self, and in the process practice the arts of application, perseverance and concentration. A new approach to education will stretch children, discover what they're capable of, and give them the joy of being in the state of flow – when they are being asked to do something which is just within their capabilities, but pushes them just beyond where they thought they could go.

We can revisit the Tomlinson recommendations and ideas from the report of the National Advisory Committee on Creative and Cultural Education *All our Futures*. We should also build on the work that the Qualifications and Curriculums Authority is doing on the future curriculum, and on initiatives such as the proposals for competency-based curricula by the Royal Society of Arts, and the emotional literacy work of Antidote. We need to improve the learning of practical knowledge and provision of vocational routes in order to build an education system which truly creates rounded young people.

A new more democratic and egalitarian approach to education and a curriculum for the twenty-first century is an essential process for creating the first generation of a good society.

8 The longevity revolution

We are living at the beginning of a revolution in ageing, a new third age of life. Life expectancy in Britain has increased dramatically, if unevenly, across the classes. The number of people aged over 65 has risen to 10.5 million, and forecasting predicts that over-65s will constitute 25 per cent of the population by 2050.

In the past ageing has been a process of becoming anonymous. Pensioned off and their labour power de-commodified, men and women were calculated to be economically without use or value. The old age pensioner was a category of welfare legislation that reduced individuals to figures of frailty and dependency.

Today there is a growing desire to live our longer lives more fully. Prejudices against older people are increasingly being challenged. Ageism in the labour market is starting to be called into question as the working age population shrinks and the retirement age is raised. The cultural revolution in ageing is an historic opportunity for older people to begin a 'whole new chapter in life' and to reject the decline into invisibility. The 'golden years of retirement' are being replaced by a new 25-30 year life stage in which education, work and leisure will exist in different proportions.

But the success of this revolution and the positive experience of the third age of life is open to question. Under present conditions, ageing for many is still a time of financial insecurity, exclusion and poverty.

In traditional societies older people embodied cultural heritage. They passed on the rules, morals and customs that governed community and family life. Our consumer culture, with its short-termism and fixation with youth, has marginalised the experience of ageing and the wisdom that comes with it. A new consumer ideology of 'successful ageing' has emerged, which encourages an individualised response to the process of growing older. Manage your body, take responsibility for your health, invest for your retirement, and the future will be 'forever young'.

This consumerist approach ignores the social realities and financial deprivations that make this kind of personal self help regime impossible for all but the wealthiest. For example, large numbers of the elderly suffer loneliness – 1.5 million over-65s are classified as socially isolated.

Contemporary anxieties about ageing are epitomised in perceptions of the care home, with its day-room of armchairs and men and women whose powerlessness and boredom seems to sap their will to live. Abuse in care homes, says the Royal College of Psychiatrists, is 'a common part of institutional life'.[27] As awareness of the problem grows, so the rates of detection and reporting will increase.[28] As well as hitting and shouting, many older people in care are subjected to the over-medication of drugs, the institutionalised deprivation of sensory feeling, and environments that generate emotional neglect and intellectual impoverishment. Finally, they suffer the lack of dignity accorded to death: less than 1 per cent of care homes ensure that the terminally ill have real control over the final stages of their lives.

More than 2.2 million pensioners are currently living below the official poverty line, the vast majority of them women. The value of the basic state pension is below the official poverty line, and a considerable shortfall on the budget necessary for basic living. In consequence, over the last five years in England and Wales between 20,000 and 50,000 people aged 65 and over have suffered avoidable winter deaths.[29] Not only is the state pension inadequate to live on; many women do not qualify for the full amount. The means-tested Pension Credit raises its value to only about £5500 a year. Private and occupational schemes are unreliable and inefficient. To compound the problem, occupational pensions that operate a defined benefit scheme are being closed. The high charges of private savings schemes, which cover a little over half the population, result in reduced pensions savings.

It is to be welcomed that government has recognised that the pensions issue needs to be dealt with. The White Paper on pensions published in 2006 is a significant step forward from the existing situation and will help deal with the poverty that many pensioners face. It will reverse the steady decline in value of the state pension by re-establishing the indexing of it to earnings. However it will postpone adoption of the earnings link until 2012 at the earliest, a further delay which will continue to reduce pensioners' promised share of future national wealth. And there is no mechanism to qualify all older women for the (inadequate) basic state pension. Instead the contributing years needed to qualify have been reduced from 39 to 30. According to the government's own projections, about a third of pensioners will still need to undergo means-testing in order to claim their full state entitlement.

Policy strategies for renewal

We believe that in the longer term, policy strategies aimed at improving the lives of the over 65s will need to be accompanied by wider changes in cultural attitudes towards ageing. A combination of cultural and economic change is needed to provide the resources to give all older citizens the chances to lead fulfilling, secure lives. The demands created by demographic shifts have profound implications for policy-makers, including for pensions, health, work and care. These shifts have generally been viewed by policy-makers as posing a threat, but we should approach them as an opportunity to review the very basis on which policy is constructed and understood.

There is a need to go further on pensions, in both the short and medium term. In the first instance, more work needs to be done to make sure that older women do get an adequate state pension. In the medium term we must make sure that the adoption of the earnings link is not postponed beyond 2012, and that pension levels are high enough in future to let people lead dignified lives. The Turner Commission on pensions noted that if sufficient increases were made to halt the decline in pensioner incomes relative to national prosperity, by 2050 there would be a gap in funding of between 3.9 per cent and 4.3 per cent of GDP. The White Paper has not moved to fill this gap in a significant way. To do so will need new kinds of taxation. Ideas for raising funds for public spending of this sort are put forward in *A New Political Economy*.

Provision for old age is not just about financial security. Policy design must address the needs of older people across a range of areas, including learning, health, work, housing and neighbourhood design, and the promotion of intergenerational understanding. As we have seen, our relationships with others are crucial to our well-being. The baby boomer generation has lower levels of social capital than previous generations, due to higher levels of divorce and separation, and from not belonging to local community structures. Social bonds, interactions and levels of participation and trust need to be strengthened. For example we need to create public spaces and neighbourhoods where people feel more comfortable interacting.

Demos has outlined a number of challenges that an ageing population raises for society and policy-makers.[30] These challenges indicate the new kinds of thinking that are required. We need to create models of economic participation that allow older people to use their skills and assets for longer. Neighbourhoods need to be redesigned to ensure older people's integration and independence, and the public realm must become better at utilising the experience of older people. We need to deal with economic insecurity and pensioner poverty and to find ways to develop a sustainable social care market based on communities. Another challenge is to meet the learning needs of older people, including improving their labour market skills. Relatedly, we should create workplaces which emphasise succession and transfer of experience rather than purely focusing upon recruitment. More broadly, we need to change communications culture so that it does not assume that life's purpose is to perpetuate youth.

Statistically speaking, we are likely to succumb to a chronic illness and end our life in a hospital, in an impersonal, possibly painful, techno-medical death. The exact character of this death and the old age that precedes it will largely be shaped by our economic status and the class we were born into. Dying in Britain today is characterised by a lack of Hospice care, a minimal understanding of palliative medicine, and a lack of opportunity to die at home. In 2005 there were only 324 palliative care doctors practicing in the NHS, with a further 100 posts unfilled, and only a few Hospice care centres, largely confined to the wealthier areas of the country. We need to improve the experience of dying, and conduct a national debate about what it means to have a good death. A national education programme could address the importance of people discussing their wishes for what is to happen to them both during the period of their dying and after death. This could promote the idea of a living will, and provide details about making one.[31]

The need to change our social and cultural life is part of the longevity revolution. To begin with, however, we must affirm our commitment to age equality. People should have equal access to participation in social life and the public realm, and equality in their life chances, regardless of their age. Government must now move to promote age equality through a mixture of regulation and better enforcement of existing legislation.

All public bodies should have a legal duty to promote age equality, as they do to promote race and gender equality. This duty would prevent defensive compliance to avoid discrimination claims in the courts. And it would help public bodies to create a systemic, joined up approach to creating age equality, one that will include employment practices as well as outcomes from public service delivery. Such a duty would create a strong equality driver in public service delivery and reform.[32]

9 Healthier lives

Health policy should aim first of all at keeping people as well as possible. Secondly it should ensure that they can get high quality, safe treatment and care when they are ill. Everyone should have access to services and facilities that enable them to safeguard and, where necessary, improve their health, regardless of their means, and regardless of their age, gender, ethnicity, location. Everyone should have an equal chance to enjoy good health and healthcare, regardless of status and circumstances. And we must recognise that this implies a need for distributing resources and services unevenly, in order to achieve more equal health outcomes and to begin to reduce health inequalities. People living in poverty need more and better services – not, as is currently the case, fewer and poorer services.

Safeguarding and improving people's health is a matter not just for health services, but for a range of services and sectors working together – education, employment, housing, benefits, transport, sport and leisure, environment. Health services as they currently stand in fact play a crucial but relatively small part in maintaining health. To set out our policies we need to start by distinguishing between health policy and health services.

Health policy is there to serve people, not clinicians or service managers. When people are asked about their 'choices' about health, they tend to go for remaining healthy and living a long, healthy life. But health policy has been so thoroughly skewed towards illness services that people are very rarely asked in such terms. They are asked about whether they would like to have a choice in what hospital they go to or, if they are lucky, what doctor or treatment they want. But we should always remember that the primary choice is to be well.

To safeguard and improve everyone's health and to tackle inequalities, we need to create the conditions that will enable everyone to 'choose' to be healthy. There are four main categories of public policy measures involved in this. The first tackles health risks that individuals cannot control themselves, whether they are rich or poor, such as, for example, air quality, climate change, traffic pollution, or the spread of drug-resistant diseases. The second tackles health risks associated with social, economic and cultural circumstances. Measures in this category are aimed at creating genuinely equal capacity to 'choose health', for example through improving education, employment, neighbourhood regeneration schemes, crime prevention, housing, civic engagement. The third policy category tackles risks arising from individual choices and lifestyles, by encouraging healthy eating, responsible drinking, taking exercise, and maintaining sexual health. The fourth is concerned with services to treat and care for people when they are ill: health and social care services.

At present, we spend a huge amount of public money on the fourth category – which is all about services. Public expectations about these services are increasingly high, ratcheted up by political leaders who make excessive claims for what a national health (or more accurately 'illness') service can achieve. We cannot sustain these arrangements. It appears that the more money we spend on illness services, the deeper the crisis becomes. Little effort is made to reduce demand by keeping people healthy.

Yet most of the major illnesses, the ones that make the biggest demands on our services, are avoidable. Obesity, for example, is a disease that is strongly associated with poverty. Poverty is associated with poor education, joblessness and social exclusion. If we can really tackle these factors, we can dramatically reduce obesity and, with it, the rates of diabetes, heart disease and other chronic conditions, which together generate a great majority of demands for services.

Policies addressing public health issues tend to focus on the third category – measures to change individual lifestyle – though the evidence strongly demonstrates that investing in this third category without also robustly investing in the second category (social, economic and cultural circumstances) only serves to widen inequalities. For a range of reasons, better off people are much more responsive than disadvantaged people to public health messages. Like education, health is becoming a 'positional good': being able to demonstrate that one has a fitter body and sounder mind has become a means by which one signals one's status in society.

New Labour began by pledging not to marketise or privatise the NHS, and reversing some Tory measures such as GP fundholding. It then made a massive funding commitment, to bring the proportion of GDP spent on health services in England up to the European average. It promised to go on pouring new money into the NHS until 2008 – a cut-off point that naturally became increasingly alarming as time went by. It focused ruthlessly on cutting waiting times and reducing premature deaths from cancer and heart disease. All this worked up to a point. Waiting times have come down and so have premature death rates from cancer and heart disease.

New Labour did not, however, tackle the power of the doctors. Much of the new money has gone on salary increases (some merited of course). There has also been a massive hospital building programme, using the private finance initiative, and this has locked the NHS into long-term spending commitments that may be based on the wrong priorities, since patterns of illness and treatment change over time. The government has also re-introduced market mechanisms into the health service, through the introduction of 'Payment by Results' and practice-based commissioning, and the encouragement of independent healthcare providers. But these measures have done nothing to significantly shift the balance of power and resources towards keeping people healthy.

The government has not seriously embraced the need to prevent illness and reduce health inequalities. It has placed more emphasis on public health than previous governments, but early efforts to produce a joined-up approach to health improvement were fatally undermined by two factors. The first was a preoccupation with clinical intervention, at the expense of thinking about preventing illness occurring in the first place. The second was a new commitment to individual choice – which has come to dominate the health policy agenda. Ministers have claimed that promoting choice is the best way not only to improve the quality of services, but also to tackle health inequalities. But these claims are not based on any convincing evidence.

The government has now recognised that long-term chronic conditions and mental health create the majority of demands for health services. It has also recognised that resources must be shifted from the acute sector to the primary and community health sector, and that the NHS has a key role to play in preventing ill health. It has taken steps to align health more closely with social care. These are positive developments. At the same time, however, it has been engulfed by problems afflicting the NHS: budget deficits, hospital acquired infections (MRSA), and the fall-out from another round of service restructuring that has created organisational confusion and the demoralisation of staff.

Policy strategies for renewal

Rather than focus on promises to create a 'world class health service', we need to create the conditions for people to lead happy, healthy lives. Instead of focusing on clinical intervention and promoting patient choice, the focus should be on sustainable development – aiming for better health for all, reducing demands for illness services by preventing avoidable illnesses, and thereby ensuring we have high quality services to treat and care for those with unavoidable illnesses.[33]

Political leadership is needed to change public understanding about what makes individuals healthy or ill, and why it makes no sense to keep on pouring public money into treatment and care without investing in measures that help reduce rates of illness. What makes people well is partly a question of diet, exercise, alcohol, drugs and sexual behaviour. But it is mainly a question of the opportunities people have through education, employment, income, social connectedness and the material environment. To develop this new approach we need to promote an understanding of the individual's role in sustaining and improving his or her own health. This would encourage people to take responsibility for safeguarding their own health. It would also encourage clinicians and patients to behave as equal partners in treating illness and managing chronic conditions. Health policy is about social justice and reducing inequality. It requires investment in decent housing and education, skills and jobs for all, and safe, clean neighbourhoods, as well as clinical interventions. Health policy is also about having access to decent food – including in hospitals!

There is mounting evidence that the mental health of the British population is deteriorating. Mental illness affects one in six people in the UK at any given time. But we are struggling to cope with it, as shown for example by the way that many mentally ill people are dumped in prison.

Good mental health underpins overall health and strongly influences behaviour, relationships, parenting, educational attainment, employment and productivity, participation in crime and quality of life. Skills and attributes associated with positive mental health (or 'flourishing') lead to improvements in these eight domains. Our prosperity and quality of life will depend on promoting and protecting the mental health and well-being of the whole population. To do this requires the development of treatment that promotes the dignity and recovery of those with mental illness.

We need higher levels of investment in dealing with mental illness and promoting mental health. This includes investment to expand the range of treatment options, to make available psychological and other non-pharmacological approaches; this would help to reduce the inequalities in access to non-pharmacological treatments. A range of therapeutic options are needed: counselling; psychotherapy; music, play and drama therapies; group analysis; cognitive behaviour therapy; and help in gaining access to convivial forms of social life. What all these have in common is a recognition that caring well for those with mental illness and lasting healing grows out of relationships, both therapeutic and social. Therapeutic help needs to be backed up by the provision of opportunities for sporting activity, self-help and education, and campaigns to improve nutrition. Equally, campaigns against alcohol and drug abuse require an infrastructure of therapeutic support, which can in part be funded by justice reinvestment – the transfer of funds from the prison system through the reduction in levels of imprisonment (see chapter four). Generally, there is a need to promote public awareness of what individuals can do to look after their mental health.

Policy in all areas – most notably criminal justice, fiscal, education, employment and early years – needs to address its impact on mental health and take into account factors that are toxic to it. These include inequalities, long working hours, imprisonment, lack of support for parenting, poor quality child care and an undue emphasis on material gain, at the expense of relationships.

10 A progressive internationalism

A good society cannot be created in one country, or in isolation from the rest of the world. It needs to be open to the world – alive to its impact on the well-being of others, as well as to the impact of others on its own well-being. Our values of equality, security, freedom, solidarity, and our recognition of cultural diversity, provide the principles necessary to create a new doctrine of internationalism for the multi-polar twenty-first century.

An unaccountable global elite is currently taking decisions that have profound implications for our lives and the future of the planet. Our society faces a world threatened by a new set of global risks: the precedent set by the use of 'pre-emptive military intervention' in Iraq, globalised forms of terrorism, extreme poverty, food and water insecurities, and massive environmental destruction.

The legitimacy of transnational institutions needs strengthening in order to set an agenda that addresses these threats. There is an urgent need for a coherent narrative that engages with these new global risks and brings together the issues of globalised communications, financial flows, trade and development, transnational institutions, security, and the environment.

Britain's own behaviour must come under our scrutiny, not least our role in supporting the US invasion of Iraq; our current military presence in Afghanistan; our arms sales to repressive regimes; and a willingness to lock ourselves into US global nuclear fighting capability by purchasing a new generation of Trident missiles.

The good society expresses itself in a progressive internationalism and foreign policy. The life force of this internationalism comes from the activities and associations of social movements and diverse cultures. These include the enormous demonstrations against the invasion of Iraq; the great range of solidarity campaigns, cultural exchanges and educational visits; people's interest in world music and arts; the anti-globalisation protests and campaigns against world poverty; groups that monitor corporate activity in less powerful countries; publications and TV programmes highlighting foreign affairs.

British citizens have ties to different national cultures, and to various kin in countries overseas, and these relationships afford the opportunity for new kinds of citizenship and solidarities that will enrich our culture and society. The creation and affirmation of new transnational cultures, identities and politics reflect new global interdependencies. They have the power to transform the territorial nature of national societies, and foster global understanding and international solidarity.

Globalisation presents a major challenge to the nation state system of government. It raises questions about the viability of a national citizenship, about belonging, and about the ways in which we define our national identity. Uncertainty and insecurity find a scapegoat in immigrants and asylum seekers. National borders become fortress-like.

And yet globalisation continues to transform nation state societies. Mass media transmits transnational public opinion with no respect for national borders. Capital markets create rapid and colossal global financial flows in and out of national economies. Migrant labour, often shunned and discriminated against, maintains the service sector in many economies. Corporations spanning continents with budgets larger than the GDP of many countries shift investment and goods within their own internal economies. Global threats such as climate change, the pre-emptive actions of the Bush administration, terrorism and the spread of AIDS and other epidemics mean that national societies are increasingly affected by events occurring outside their borders.

The good society needs to address the interrelationship between the global and local, and build democratic and accountable transnational institutions of global governance, that promote human security, fair trade and a decent life for all.[34] Four significant problems are driving the world towards ever greater levels of poverty, violence and insecurity. First, many countries and regions are failing to move towards the United Nations Millennium Development Goals, which set the minimum humanitarian levels for large sections of the world population. Second, there is an institutional failure to resolve serious questions about the regulation of world trade and the redress of global inequality. Third, despite global warming threatening the existence of human life on earth, there is a failure to establish an adequate collective global response. Fourth, there is an erosion of the multilateral order, symbolised by the United Nations but extending through a whole series of international agreements and agencies.

The post-war multilateral order is threatened by the intersection and combination of these humanitarian, economic, environmental and political crises. More serious still, there is a driving force taking them from bad to worse. This force can be summed up in two phrases: the Washington economic consensus and the Washington security strategy. The economic consensus is characterised by free trade, capital market liberalisation, secure property rights, deregulation, and the transfer of assets from the public to the private sectors. It has been the economic orthodoxy for most of the last twenty years in leading OECD countries, and during that time the IMF and World Bank have prescribed it, until recently without qualification, as the only policy basis for less industrialised countries. The evidence is now clear that the Washington consensus has served the interests of the US, and that its economic orthodoxies have failed to generate sustained economic growth, poverty reduction or fair outcomes in many of the poorer parts of the world.

The US and its major allies have systematically failed to strengthen international law and enhance the role of multilateral institutions in the face of global terrorism. Since 9/11 the world has become more polarised, and international law has become weaker. The systematic political failings of the Washington consensus have been compounded by the Washington security strategy, at the heart of which is the doctrine of unilateral and pre-emptive war. This security strategy contradicts most of the core tenets of international politics and international agreements since 1945, and throws aside respect for political negotiations among states. It heralds a return to the view of international relations as, in the last analysis, a 'war of all against all'. Once this 'freedom' is granted to the US, why not also to Russia or China; India or Pakistan; North Korea or Iran? It cannot be consistently argued that all states bar one must accept limits on their self-defined goals, and that this can be called law. It will not take long for such an approach to become manifestly counter-productive.

Policy strategies for renewal

In place of the Washington Consensus and Washington Security Strategy we need a framework of global governance. It must be one that can sustain the enormous enhancement of productivity and wealth that the market and contemporary technology make possible and ensure that its benefits are fairly shared. To create a good society will mean not only addressing national inequalities, but also the extremes of global poverty and wealth. This would be part of our commitment to international security. By engaging with the causes as well as the crimes of terrorism, war and failed states, we will also enhance our own security and well-being.

There is a need for a new global security agenda. It will require three things of governments and international institutions – all currently missing. First, there must be a commitment to the rule of law and the development of multilateral institutions that can prosecute a robust form of international law enforcement. Second, a sustained effort has to be undertaken to generate new forms of global political legitimacy for international institutions involved in security and peacemaking. Third, there must be a head-on acknowledgment that the ethical and justice issues posed by the global polarisation of wealth, income and power, and with them the huge asymmetries of life-chances, cannot be left to markets to resolve.

The four major interlocking crises of the multilateral order are evidence of the current lack of political will to confront some of the most pressing global threats. The economic resources do exist to put in place reforms to aid the world's least well-off. The question really is about how we allocate our resources, to whose benefit and to what end.

There are a wide number of interventions to promote a progressive internationalism. We need to revisit Robin Cook's notion of an 'ethical foreign policy' and develop what this means in practice. We must rethink our relationship with the US. We need to accept that the gains that are made from the 'special relationship' are outweighed by the costs to our relationships with other partners, especially in Europe, and to our freedom to act in a more principled fashion. We also need to be clearer about when it is appropriate to suspend the norm of non-intervention and to intervene in another country's affairs – e.g. in the case of genocide. The fact that the intervention in Iraq was not done on the grounds of clear principle is a major source of the erosion of trust in the government.

A New Political Economy considers many of the economic aspects of a progressive internationalism, such as trade, aid and debt. But the good society is not based on just good economics. We must promote peace, for example through investing in failing states and enforcing rigorous arms control. It is estimated that there is one gun for every ten people on the planet. We support the campaign by Amnesty International and others for a global arms trade treaty. This will prevent the sale of weapons which are likely to be used in abuse of human rights, and will provide the means to pressure states to be transparent about who they sell arms to.

New forms of global governance are explored in both the two other Compass Programme for Renewal books. They suggest ways in which international bodies, such as the IMF, World Bank and WTO, can be made more effective and democratic. We need to strengthen the United Nations by dealing with underlying issues not symptoms – particularly its funding. We should also recognise that Europe is the obvious first global building block for Britain in its approach to the major international problems that we face.

The major issue of our time is the environment. It connects up to all of the other key issues we face: poverty (the poorest tend to live in the most vulnerable environments); security (climate change is the biggest security threat we face); and migration (there are increasing numbers of environmental refugees). The environment shows our interdependence, and we can only tackle environmental issues together. Global institutions which promote financial and economic interests need to be checked and balanced by global institutions promoting social and environmental interests. A new institution – a World Environmental Organisation – could promote the implementation of existing environmental agreements and treaties. Its main mission would be to ensure that the development of world trading and financial systems is compatible with the sustainable use of the world's resources. It is only by creating modern democratic institutions of global governance, capable of dealing with today's global issues, that we can move towards a good society for all.

11 Immigration and asylum seekers

In Britain, immigration has been seen as an example of the difficult and tempestuous problems created by globalisation. Our society, dominated by the values of acquisitiveness, self interest, and winner-takes-all, lacks a public ethic of hospitality.

Inequality fosters resentment and an impoverishment of goodwill toward the needs of immigrants. Immigrants are seen as taking jobs and lowering wages, even though research shows that higher immigration seems to be linked to higher wages for the UK-born workforce.[35] Asylum seekers need resources and they need help, and so attract envy, rage and suspicion. They have become scapegoats for widespread feelings of insecurity. Popular anger over immigration is fuelled by the right-wing media, and the idea that the British way of life is under threat. 'Foreigners' are accused of making 'unjustified claims' on health, welfare and education resources. This language of fear, suspicion and disappointment has been harnessed by the British National Party, as it seeks to legitimise its claim to represent a disenfranchised, indigenous white population.

In response to popular xenophobia, there has been an argument from some who count themselves as liberals that the growing diversity of British society is threatening to undermine its social cohesion, together with the values of solidarity that underpin the welfare state. They argue that if values become more diverse, if lifestyles become more differentiated, it becomes more difficult to sustain the legitimacy of a universal risk-pooling welfare state. People will ask: 'Why should I pay for them when they are doing things that I wouldn't do?' But this is to raise the very same question that the wealthy have repeatedly and insistently asked throughout the history of the welfare state. There have always been differences within British society – for example between regions, nations, classes and genders. It is impossible to base social cohesion on the absence of difference. And it is economic inequality, not ethnic difference, which is the main driver of social injustice, which aggravates religious and cultural division. Ideological appeals to uphold the interests of race and nation are a means of managing the internal divisions of a society, and evading the sources of the problems.

For working-class people living in areas of scarce employment opportunities, the arrival of immigrants from Eastern Europe willing to work for lower wages heightens their insecurity and fear of unemployment. A similar anxiety exists where there is a scarcity of affordable public housing.

Rather than confront the xenophobia and social consequences of its own deregulated labour market, New Labour has backed away from both problems. Immigration and asylum have been discussed in populist terms by politicians, misrepresented by the media and mismanaged at the level of policy, and this has created shameful and cruel conditions for migrants, asylum seekers and their children. Rather than grapple with the problems of the trend towards a more cosmopolitan society, New Labour's agenda has been dominated by the promotion of narrow ideas of national identity and calls for the teaching of 'traditional British values'.

New Labour has attempted to re-orientate policy on immigration by the introduction of 'managed migration' and strategies for integration and the promotion of social cohesion. At the core of its initiatives is the conviction that Britain's ability to compete in global markets, and its understanding of itself as a modern country, requires proactive immigration policies which facilitate the movement of large numbers of people across national frontiers.

However, though it accepts the economic case for immigration, the government has taken little responsibility for the well-being of migrants, or for the welcome they receive. Government coordination of migration activities has been confined to the highest levels of government and administration, and key stakeholders amongst employers in the private and public sectors. It has not made a serious effort to work in conjunction with grassroots, community-based organisations to build a wider consensus in support of progressive immigration policies. In fact there is plenty of evidence that it considers the efforts of organisations representing the rights of immigrants to be 'off message' and generally unwelcome. It has operated under the assumption that the tabloid representation of a profoundly prejudiced public opinion against immigrants is accurate. It has assumed that it can do little other than to appease anxiety and apprehension. Its frequent proclamations on immigration policy are governed by one fundamental theme: despite granting entry to those who can demonstrate by their utility to business that they are needed, a control and enforcement machine ensures that all the unwanted immigrants are kept out.

The government has failed to ease the obvious pressures on local GPs, dentists, schools and housing services where immigrants have been located. This is a major reason for rising social tensions in some communities.

There has been a failure to address public anxiety. The government has found that the strict control component of its public message has been transformed into the yardstick by which all immigration is judged. This has affected the admission rights of highly skilled workers, the family members of people settled in the UK, and refugees in need of humanitarian protection. Even the welcome decision to admit citizens of the new European Union accession countries after May 2004 was allowed to develop into a major controversy, despite the clear evidence that they would fill labour market gaps and actively contribute to the economy.

Eight years after New Labour began its fundamental reform of immigration policy, many migrants have been pushed into positions of marginality and exposed to harshly exploitative working conditions. Low levels of public support for their welfare, and new forms of racism directed against 'abusive asylum seekers' have increased their difficulties, as they subsist in low skill, casualised sectors of the economy.

Policy strategies for renewal

People in Britain can be won over to the idea that our welfare and prosperity increasingly requires the free movement of workers and skilled professionals across the globe. We need managed migration, but we need not be afraid of it. The gains of the last few decades in pushing racism and discrimination out of large parts of society need to be replicated in dealings with migrant workers. Respect for basic human rights should underpin all immigration policies, and the argument must be made that living in a multicultural society has the potential to bring benefits to all citizens.

One line of argument which could help here is drawing attention to the connection between falling European populations, future pensions liabilities and the need for increased immigration to fill the economic shortfall. And more work needs to be done to manage the effects of the process of migration upon existing communities. Whilst the middle classes tend to welcome immigration for the cheap labour that it provides, people who are against immigration are more likely to come from the white working class. Their fears about the impacts on their communities, services and jobs need to be actively addressed by policy-makers. We need to directly counter the myth that immigration is depressing wages for low paid workers.

We presently have over half a million illegal immigrants in the UK and we need a strategy to deal with them. We must accept that they will not easily be deported and need to consider practical solutions. We should consider the regularisation scheme proposed by the Joint Council for the Welfare of Immigrants. This would be a programme where migrants who have been living in the UK for seven years without a serious criminal record should be allowed to stay. Those here for at least two years could apply for temporary leave to remain and be eligible to apply for permanency at a later date. This kind of managed amnesty would help service-planners, who are presently having to make estimates about delivery in the absence of accurate knowledge of the numbers who are living in any given place. It would also add to the income of the Treasury through the higher tax take.

Migrant and refugee community organisations should be brought into the mainstream of civic and public life in the UK. This would enable the formulation of policies to involve the active participation of all stakeholders, and not just the business elites. This process could be a part of a wider encouragement to learn English and other skills. The trade union movement can help to bring migrant workers into the scope of their activities. Policies for the management of economic migration should take full account of the human rights of workers and members of their families, and guarantee protection in the workplace against exploitative practices. There needs to be a thorough review of all aspects of immigration policies to ensure that they do not discriminate against women or place them in positions where they are marginal and vulnerable to abuse.

Over the longer-term, there has to be a fundamental re-orientation of immigration policies, one which acknowledges the right of the governments of immigrant-sending countries to participate as equal partners in the formulation of policies which affect their nationals. In particular there needs to be more exploration of how to recompense poor countries for the investment they have made in people such as doctors and teachers who leave for richer ones, creating a 'brain drain' for those who can least afford it. There is potential within the European Union for the formulation and implementation of progressive immigration policies, and this needs developing. Lastly, an international structure is required – a World Migration Organisation under the auspices of the United Nations – which would have oversight and direction over global immigration policies.

To improve the lives of migrants and asylum seekers, domestic policies on migration and asylum must conform to international standards. Policies on refugees must be based on strict adherence to the standards of the Geneva Convention on the Status of Refugees and its Protocols, the European Convention on Human Rights, and other international agreements guaranteeing protection to all in fear of persecution and inhuman treatment. The UK should accede to the Council of Europe's Trafficking Convention, which gives rights to trafficked people. The UK should also become a signatory to the International Convention of the Rights of Migrant Workers and their Families. Politicians need to support popular campaigns and help create the space to push forward such proposals. They need to be braver in making the case that asylum is a human right and that migration is beneficial to society.

12 Racism and cultural differences

Britain is becoming a society that is increasingly divided along the lines of race and religion. We are becoming more unequal by ethnicity. Racism remains a significant problem, as most overtly illustrated by the electoral successes of the British National Party. In terms of race relations Britain is unique in its diversity of racial backgrounds and in its legislation that promotes race equality. However, like many other countries, the UK is struggling to meet the demands of ensuring equality and at the same time tackling the challenges – many of them global – posed by the changed dynamics of race and culture. Some of these challenges are illustrated by recent disturbances in Paris, the 7/7 London bombings, the tragic events in New Orleans, and the increasingly blurred lines between freedom of speech and incitement to hatred.

In the face of these events the call for community cohesion can carry a coded meaning of denying inequalities. Success is defined as the absence of open conflict in the streets. But, by the time we get to the violence, we will have gone way beyond the situation we needed to address. Do we want to live in a society where, as in one local authority area in the West Midlands, large numbers of parents refuse to allow their children to go on educational visit to a mosque because of a claim that it was 'run by Al Qaeda'?

Racism is inextricably linked with the inequality of ethnic minorities. The causes of this inequality have changed over the past twenty years. While the number of reported racial incidents is falling slightly and blatant discrimination or harassment is not found as frequently as in the past, other forms of racism are prevalent. Non-whites systematically experience poorer outcomes across a range of indicators, including education, health, employment and political representation. They are more than six times more likely to be stopped and searched than white people. And, according to government figures, two thirds of the UK's ethnic minorities live in the poorest areas and worst housing in the country.

Residential isolation is increasing for many minority groups, especially

South Asians. Some minorities are moving into middle-class, less ethnically concentrated areas, but those who are left behind are hardening in their separateness. The number of people of Pakistani heritage in what are technically called 'ghetto' communities trebled between 1991 and 2001; 13 per cent live in such communities in Leicester (the figure was 10.8 per cent in 1991) and 13.3 per cent in Bradford (4.3 per cent in 1991). Children are slightly more segregated in the playground than they are in their neighbourhoods. Recent research in one London borough's primary schools showed that 17 schools had more than 90 per cent Bangladeshi pupils, while nine others had fewer than 10 per cent.[36]

Alongside this type of geographical segregation, communities increasingly inhabit separate social, religious and cultural worlds. Ethnic minority communities can find themselves culturally and sometimes even physically ring-fenced within cities. In these segregated neighbourhoods, they can feel intimidated and under siege, and neighbouring majority communities can also feel excluded, so the two simply never interact.

For many second and third generation migrants, increased resort to more traditional forms of identification such as religion has arisen out of the encounter with western modernity and western lifestyles. For example the 'return to Islam' is borne out of disenchantment with Enlightenment modernity – the weakening of a sense of belonging and community in the face of individualisation and consumer lifestyles. Traditional forms of identification are being drawn upon to restore a sense of stability. Tradition and religion are not being uncritically embraced however; instead the meanings of, for example, Islam or being Asian are being renegotiated and redefined. These 'migrant' identities provide alternative conceptions of the 'good life' and a critique of western modernity.

It is likely that there will always be geographical concentrations of particular groups. This will be due to the economic and emotional interdependence of families (particularly amongst new immigrants), and a shared culture or religion which requires proximity to places of worship, community organisations or, more prosaically, shops selling particular kinds of foods. The geographical segregation of communities should not be seen as the enemy of integration. Equally, however, it should not be allowed to develop into enclaves of economic deprivation and social segregation.

For the idea of Britishness to succeed we must seek common equal citizenship that promotes a sense of belonging, so that all groups feel at home.

Citizenship must be based on a differentiated form of solidarity, one that does not reduce everyone to a singular identity. It must allow for the affirmation of cultural difference and develop a global dimension. For this to succeed we have to address the failures of some of the earlier antiracist and multicultural strategies. These did not address serious and systemic racial and class disadvantages.

We need to address the complexities of cultural difference. For example, discussions of race and religion tend to leave gender out of the equation, except where women symbolise the oppression of 'the community.' This can lead to a situation where women find themselves oppressed from both outside and within their communities.

Policy strategies for renewal

There is still substantial work to be done to ensure that people's life chances are not adversely affected by their race or religion. The absolute precondition for a more integrated society is equality. Most ethnic minority Britons are poorer, less well educated, less healthy and less politically engaged than their white counterparts.

We need to devise policies to tackle the high levels of unemployment that exist amongst ethnic minorities. All minority groups have higher unemployment than whites, and in certain localities the problems are severe – for example 70 per cent of young Bangladeshis in Tower Hamlets are unemployed. Solutions to these problems will need a range of measures, such as clear employment targets for the private sector, more targeted work to improve skills amongst ethnic minorities, and efforts to ensure that race equality outcomes form part of value-for-money assessment in government procurement.

Health outcomes are poorer for ethnic minorities than whites and they often suffer institutionalised racism. For example African Caribbeans are 40 per cent more likely to be turned away by mental health services than a white person. Infant mortality rates are twice as high in the Pakistani and Caribbean communities as they are among whites. We need to eradicate these health inequalities through tackling inequality more broadly, as described in chapter two, and through assessing the performance of health institutions against this measure.

Political representation of ethnic minorities is shockingly low, with representation at local authority level estimated at less than 3 per cent, and at Westminster being even lower than this. If we continued at the pace of change we have had thus far, it is not until 2150 that ethnic minorities would be proportionately represented in the House of Commons. Political parties should undertake a race audit of their membership and staff, and develop comprehensive programmes to recruit and promote ethnic minorities within their parties. There should be far greater opening up of our democratic structures to diverse communities, in order to make everybody feel that these are their institutions and that they can be part of them.

The problem of segregation is not assisted by some of the public discussion that has taken place about the definition of 'Britishness' as a way of creating a more integrated society. The political vision and language here has been disappointing, tending to veer towards a more assertive and narrowly conceived British identity. We need to advocate a solidarity and acknowledgement of interdependency that is not simply confined to proposals for an inward-looking national integration.

To help evolve a collective and cosmopolitan idea of Britishness, there needs to be a serious historical accounting of Empire. The failure to account for its complex influence leads to a lack of understanding of the crisis of British, and specifically white English, identity. There is a need to assess the role of Empire in constructing modern Britain's racism as well as its domestic multicultural politics. For example, any understanding of Britain's role in a new politics of US-led imperialism has to engage seriously with its own imperial history. There are aspects of current New Labour and government policy discourse that echo older colonial formulations, reconstructed and modified to meet the demands of twenty-first century threats to social order.

We need to develop an idea of national identity that provides an alternative to the superficial and prescriptive approach evident in calls for a Britishness day. Our sense of belonging, whether local, national or global, is never singular and without contradiction. It is possible to be British, and also to support different interests – and national or local sporting teams – at different times, without forsaking one's sense of belonging to the country. Alternative versions of national identity need to embrace the differences between us. Our right to citizenship should not be based on being either 'in' or 'out'.

A new conception of citizenship should not be seen in terms of a choice between an inaccurate history of shared identity, an 'anything-goes' relativism, or a racialised, Eurocentric superiority. We can build on a framework of human rights as a minimum conception of citizenship. The tie that can bind us together is living in a society where we respect people's rights. As a society, we share a concern that people are treated fairly and equally before the law, are given free trials and have their privacy respected. Such a concept of citizenship is one that most of us can rally round; and it would enable us to be clearer about when boundaries have been crossed. The good society needs such a notion of citizenship – balancing diversity and solidarity, individual autonomy and collective endeavour.

13 The environment we inhabit

Our hopes for the good society are dependent upon changing our relationship to the earth and to nature. A mere two hundred years of industrial production and consumption by a fraction of the human population has brought us to the limit of the planet's carrying capacity. Today, if everyone in the world consumed natural resources and emitted carbon dioxide at the rate we do in Europe we would need three planets to sustain us.

We are approaching the 'topping-out point' of oil – the peak of production. Once reached, the price of oil will begin to climb sky high, bringing with it the threat of economic chaos. A week was once described as a long time in politics. We have to begin measuring political time in terms of hundreds, even thousands, of years if we are to sustain and improve human life on earth.

Ecological sustainability is the inescapable reality facing the good society. But we cannot approach the environment separately from our other values. We need to move towards sustainable development that is also based on equity, health and democracy. The most powerful model for this comes from the Rio Earth Summit, which called for a Local Agenda for the 21st Century. This was based on the democratic involvement of local communities to create change towards sustainable development.

There is a broad consensus of agreement amongst world scientists that human activities have increased the atmospheric concentrations of greenhouse gases and aerosols since the pre-industrial era.[37] In response to the dangers of climate change government has set a target to reduce greenhouse gas emissions by 60 per cent by 2050. However it is not on course to achieve this, and a growing body of evidence suggests that markedly faster and deeper cuts are needed for climate security. Many of the changes needed over the next thirty years are well understood – both in the rich world, which has so far contributed most to emissions, and in the poorer countries whose emissions are growing fast. We do not have to wait for major technical breakthroughs to make deep cuts in emissions. We know that there is already huge scope for change: through reducing demand and increasing the efficiency of our energy and water consumption; reducing our dependence on the car through the use of alternative transport or telecommunications; investing far more in renewable energy supplies; and soaking up carbon through the planting and maintenance of forests.

Ecological sustainability is about social justice; it is not about the affluent – the biggest polluters – buying their way out of their obligations. The changes that are needed require a combination of individual and collective action, and this in turn requires the solidarity of individuals who feel that they are all in the same boat. We do not have this at the moment, and consequently the government response – to climate change, to the depletion of fossil fuels, to the growing scarcity of water – is enfeebled and patchy. If we are going to survive as a species, let alone build a good society, we are going to need determination, imagination, collective energy and the individual desire to change our ways of life.

The resource we need to build up rapidly is political willpower and commitment. Government has to be forced into action in order to engage both business and households in achieving environmental goals, including reduction in energy and water use, and waste generation. Individuals need persuading out of their cars. Cycle paths and footpaths are needed. Landscape, biodiversity and air quality need protecting. Measures are required for reducing levels of noise pollution. Electricity and water companies need to be forced to waste less and people encouraged to conserve water.

Awareness and concern about environmental issues is growing, and most people take limited action, such as recycling newspapers. However, few look at the environmental performance of their household in a systematic way. As consumers we adopt behaviour patterns that we find difficult to change. To help us make these changes we need a culture of solidarity and an integrated approach by government which operates at all levels, linking policy measures with information.

Policy strategies for renewal

The policy strategies are primarily based around changes we can all make as individuals with the help of government and business. Both *A New Political Economy* and *Democracy and the Public Realm* consider the implications of environmental change for regulation, tax, business and government.

The report *Towards Sustainable Consumption: 'I will if you will'*, produced by the National Consumer Council and the Sustainable Development Commission, identifies four areas of our lives that generate most of our overall impact on our environment.[38] These are the food we eat, our holidays, our transport and our homes. Our approach and policy recommendations follow that report. Some of the policies that we put forward may seem relatively minor in the face of a large problem, but they are indicative of an approach which is focused on creating behaviour change amongst people, and which aims to open up spaces for further political change.

With the support of government and business we can tackle each of these aspects of our lives, beginning with small changes that require relatively little of us, and opening the way to changes that ask us to alter our habits and routines, for example through switching to eating foods that are in season, turning off lights, or walking rather than driving.

As consumers we are keen to act on environmental issues, but often feel that any efforts we might make would be isolated and in vain. Rather than waiting on individuals to make decisions on complex environmental problems, government and business should create the conditions that would make the pro-environmental choice the easy choice. Making these smaller changes can help lead us to rethinking aspects of our lifestyle – what we aspire to owning or having, and what it is about them that makes us want them. Changing our consumer practice is in part about its ecological and social impact, but it could also be motivated by a different understanding of self-interest. Many of the important pleasures in life are being lost because of the negative aspects of our high speed, work dominated, materialistic life-style. Our affluent consumption has been compromised by its unpleasurable by-products – noise, pollution, danger, stress, health risks, excessive waste, and aesthetic impact on the environment. We need to develop alternative forms of hedonism.

The food we eat is the average household's biggest impact on climate change, responsible for 31 per cent of our carbon emissions. Intensive factory farming is becoming increasingly costly in terms of pollution, decreasing nutritional value, food poisoning, and the growing threat of disease and epidemics. Total global meat demand is expected to grow to 327m tonnes by 2020. This increased demand will require a vast quantity of extra land, water, feed and chemicals, more transport for its distribution, and more resources for its processing and packaging. At the end of this chain, the average household throws away more than three kilograms of food and 14 kilograms of food packaging each week.

We can buy food with as little packaging as possible, compost waste, cut down on meat and dairy produce. We can avoid eating over-exploited white fish like cod. The fish we eat are disappearing from the seas. 70 per cent of global fish stocks are fished to their limit or over-fished. Buying less processed food, which is often high in fats, salt and sugar, will also contribute to improving our health. We can avoid air-freighted fruit and vegetables, instead buying local seasonal produce. Where we buy from is also important – we might shop at local markets, eat organic foods, support farmers' markets and local agricultural produce.

Government has a major role to play in helping to promote changes in our eating habits through policy strategies around poverty, inequality and primary health care. We need to introduce healthy meals and sustainable, and where possible organic, foods into schools and hospitals. Strategies of healthy eating need to be part of a broader approach to food production and economic development. There are regions and localities that are fresh food deserts. The planning system should be used to ensure equitable access to fresh fruit and vegetables. Investment is needed in organic agriculture and in developing sustainable rural economies. Food co-operatives can provide good quality food at lower prices for people on low incomes.

Choosing ecological sustainability is an opportunity for new pleasures, better nutrition and improved health. It involves promoting sustainable forms of agriculture, which do not include intensive factory farming or systemic cruelty to animals. An example of a new kind of cultural politics based on such concerns is the Slow Food movement, set up in Italy in 1986. Today it has over 80,000 members in 100 countries. It is an attempt to preserve local food cultures, promote good living and the pleasure of eating, and challenge the power and influence of multinational food producers.

The quality of the food we eat is closely linked to our well-being. Foods high in salt, fats and sugar play a significant part in the epidemic of obesity and heart disease. There is a growing body of evidence linking convenience foods, trans fats and processed meats to poor mental health, particularly in children. The brain relies on good nutrition. Improving the national diet would be a major social investment in health, longevity and living well. Government should work closely with the Audit Commission to ensure that councils, schools and hospitals are enabled to serve meals that are both healthy and sustainably produced. The example set by these should have spill-over effects onto what we as parents, pupils and patients assume is a healthy diet for ourselves at home.

The British made a record 9 million holiday trips abroad in 2004, an increase from 6.7 million in 1971.[39] Many of us want to take short breaks and fly abroad for the sun. Low cost flights are viewed as an opportunity for the less well off to travel abroad. In fact the poorest quarter of society took only 10 per cent of the flights in 2005. More than half the passengers on budget airlines come from the wealthiest quarter of the population, often those with second homes, who average six return flights a year.

On present trends air flight will contribute to more than half of the UK's share of greenhouse gases by 2050. Expanding the aviation industry is not consistent with meeting the UK's target of 60 per cent reduction in carbon. Yet the government is currently set to carry out the biggest single programme of aviation expansion ever, aiming to supply facilities to allow a growth in passenger numbers from the current 25 million annually to 82 million by 2030. The new Terminal 5 now being built at Heathrow is central to this plan. We need to reverse this trend and use alternative modes of transport, and to travel abroad less often. Cutting the carbon emissions created by air travel has to begin with creating a popular awareness of the problem. As a start on facilitating behaviour change, government should give airlines a clear incentive to introduce good quality carbon offsetting on an opt-out basis. This will help people connect cheap flights with carbon change, which will then make it easier for government to introduce further necessary reforms in the area, some of which are detailed in *A New Political Economy*.

Our use of energy for appliances and heating and lighting our homes is responsible for 28 per cent of our climate change impact. It is difficult for us to translate the idea of energy into our everyday domestic habits. Developing policies around micro-generation is a way of engaging householders in making changes and reducing levels of carbon waste. Technologies like solar water heating, mini wind turbines and air source heat pumps can change people's attitudes toward energy use at home, and are also a significant new sector of economic activity.

The 2006 Budget provided £50m to enable 30,000 buildings in Britain (0.15 per cent of its building stock) to micro-generate some of their own electricity. This figure has to be compared with the billions of pounds being spent by countries like Japan and Germany on support programmes for developing solar PV. Loft and cavity wall insulation, which creates significant energy savings, received a £20m investment, given to local authorities to improve the insulation of 250,000 homes. This amounts to only £87 per home. The government needs to make a major investment in the growing economic sector of sustainable technologies and renewable energy. Government should seek to roll out micro-renewables on new and existing homes and schools. This will help people make a personal connection between energy use and climate change, again making other measures in relation to energy more feasible.

On a more macro scale we should follow the inspiring lead of Sweden on energy and resource policy. Sweden set up a Commission on Oil Independence in 2005, under the leadership of its prime minister, which has reviewed how to end the country's dependence on oil by 2020. This kind of radical thinking is required in the UK, and we should set up a similar process to consider how to handle the challenges ahead.

Consumer culture glorifies speed. The ideas of 'progress' and 'development' have become more or less synonymous with those of saving time or speeding up, to the point where it is now well-nigh impossible to travel any long distance other than by air. Cars are the symbol of individualism and modernity. They provide personal status and autonomy and are a source of pleasure. However their social cost is becoming unacceptably high. Their promise of mobility is frequently undermined by the sheer weight of traffic on the roads, which ratchets up the demand for new roads, so destroying tracts of the countryside and serving only to increase car use. The sheer speed of road traffic is responsible for bringing premature and horrific death to many. In this country alone, over 4000 children and 8000 adults are killed or seriously injured every year while walking or cycling, by cars or lorries.

One aim of transport policy has to be to facilitate the movement of people at an affordable price. But a second aim must be to attempt to limit and reduce the damaging environmental effects of transport. It is not enough to simply encourage the construction of large amounts of public transport infrastructure in order to make society as a whole more mobile. New facilities eat up considerable energy resources. For example a high-speed line between London and the north is not necessarily an environmentally friendly option.

The key is to have a policy strategy which is not transport-maximising but instead focuses upon access. Policies should be geared wherever possible to damping down demand. This must start with the planning system. The out of town shopping centres that planners have allowed over the last three decades have an enormous and ongoing impact on the environment and on the demand for car use. So does the creation of huge district hospitals and large comprehensives. Planning policies need to take into account transport demand over the lifetime of a scheme, and favour environmentally-friendly forms of transport.

The Congestion Charge introduced by Mayor of London Ken Livingstone is a good example of brave politics creating popular appeal. The logic of dampening demand through a tax, but investing the proceeds in public transport, is faultless and should be extended to the heart of other major cities.

We need to find the best mechanisms to protect the environment and promote social and economic well-being. Much can be done through market mechanisms. Road traffic growth slowed dramatically during the period of the fuel tax escalator and has also been reduced since oil prices started soaring in 2005. Similarly, the rapid rise in air travel has been stimulated by the cheapness of air fares, and yet the aviation industry makes virtually no contribution to the alleviation of the substantial environmental damage it is causing, since its fuel is untaxed and there is only a modest tax on each flight. Overall, there must be more emphasis on the local in transport policy. Facilitating local travel is especially important for groups on low incomes who rely on public transport. On the national scale, the solution has to be demand management.[40]

Climate change is an epochal challenge but one which we can meet by advancing policy strategies for ecological sustainability on both national and supranational levels. We need to tackle environmental challenges in ways that meet our other values. Changes must be equitable and democratic, and promote health and well-being. We need to develop renewable decentralised sources of energy, a collective, global husbandry of fresh water, and a rational and fair system of agricultural production, trade and distribution of food. We need to establish a new kind of relationship between the natural world and the civic cultures, economic priorities and jurisprudence of society. At the heart of ecological sustainability is a recognition of the constraints placed on us by the earth. We have to significantly reduce the burning of carbon rich fuels. We must stop cutting down forests and catching fish at a rate at which they cannot be replenished. We have to stop throwing away the colossal amount of waste and packaging that is overwhelming our land fill sites, and being shipped overseas and dumped in the poorest countries of the world. Instead of exporting the pollution and environmental damage created by economic growth to poorer countries, we will have to work together to create forms of economic development and growth that are carbon-free and which do not lay waste to both society and the natural world.

These constraints do not necessarily mean a loss of opportunity and individuality, nor do they mean a social regime of denial and prescription. They provide the opportunity for social change, for political renewal and economic innovation; for a society which is less centred on consumption and materialist values and more focused upon the quality of living.

Afterword

We give the last word to the founder of neo-liberalism Friedrich von Hayek, who offers us a lesson for the future:

'The main lesson which the true liberal must learn from the success of the socialists is that it was their courage to be Utopian which gained them the support of the intellectuals and thereby an influence on public opinion.'

Notes

1. The Sainsbury Centre for Mental Health, www.scmh.org.uk. See also, Richard Layard, 'Mental Health: Britain's Biggest Social Problem?', www.strategy.gov.uk/downloads/files/mh_layard.pdf.

2. See Will Paxton, *Wealth Distribution – the evidence*, Institute for Public Policy Research (IPPR) 2002, www.ippr.org.uk.

3. For research on poverty and inequality in Britain see for example: Will Paxton and Mike Dixon, *The State of the Nation: An Audit of Injustice in the UK*, IPPR 2004, www.ippr.org.uk; Holly Sutherland, Tom Sefton and David Piachaud, *Poverty in Britain The impact of government policy since 1997*, Joseph Rowntree Foundation, www.jrf.org.uk; National Statistics, 'Share of the Wealth', www.statistics.gov.uk; James Banks, Zoe Smith, Matt Wakefield, 'The Distribution of Financial Wealth in the UK: Evidence from 2000 BHPS Data, Institute of Fiscal Studies', www.ifs.org.uk; Mike Brewer et al, 'Poverty and Inequality in Britain: 2004', *Commentary 96*, www.ifs.org.uk.

4. The Fawcett Society, *A Manifesto for Equality*, 2004, www.fawcettsociety.org.uk.

5. For information on ethnic minorities and inequality see Campaign for Racial Equality at www.cre.gov.uk/research/index.html.

6. Disability Rights Alliance and Centre for Research in Social Policy at Loughborough University, 'Disabled People's Cost of Living', 2004, www.disabilityalliance.org/poverty6.htm.

7. Crime and Society Foundation, *Criminal Obsessions*, 2005.

8. Richard Webber, Tim Butler, *Classifying Pupils by where they live: How well does this predict variations in their GCSE results?*, Centre for Advanced Spatial Analysis, 2006, www.casa.ucl.ac.uk/working_papers/paper99.pdf.

9. Jo Blanden, Paul Gregg and Stephen Machin, *Intergenerational Mobility in Europe and North America*, Centre for Economic Performance, April 2005, http://cep.lse.ac.uk/

10. See Richard Wilkinson's work on the relationship between inequality and health. For example: Richard Wilkinson, 'The impact of inequality: empirical evidence', *Renewal*, Vol. 14, No.1, 2006, www.renewal.org.uk.

11. Women's Budget Group, www.wbg.org.uk.

12. D. Hirsch, *What will it take to end child poverty?*, Joseph Rowntree Foundation, 2006.

13. For the statistics in this section see Prison Reform Trust, *Bromley Briefings*, April 2006; also the joint Treasury/Home Office review which has formed the basis of justice policy since it was published: Patrick Carter, *Managing Offenders, Reducing Crime*, Strategy Unit 2003, www.noms.homeoffice.gov.uk/downloads/Pat_Carter_Review.pdf.

14. See for example, William Higham, 'Punishment and Social Justice', in Ben Shimson (ed), *Social Justice: Criminal Justice,* The Smith Institute, www.smith-institute.org.uk/pdfs/social-justice_criminal-justice.pdf.

15. See Madeleine Bunting, *Willing Slaves: How the Overwork Culture is Ruling our Lives*, Harper Perennial 2005.

16. 'Mind, stress and mental health in the workplace', May 2005, www.mind.org.uk.

17. The Employer's Forum, *Age at Work*, 2005, www.efa.org.uk.

18. Ashley Seager, '£250k a year? GPs were better off in '66', *Guardian*, 22 April 2006.

19. Catherine Howarth and Peter Kenway, *Why worry any more about the Low Paid*, New Policy Institute 2004, www.npi.org.uk/reports/low%20pay.pdf.

20. Derek Wanless, *Securing Good Care for Older People*, 2006, www.kingsfund.org.uk/publications.

21. For further work on the ethic of care see Susan Himmelweit, *Can we afford (not) to care: prospects and policy*, Gender Institute, New Working Papers issue 15, LSE, 2005, www.lse.ac.uk/collections/GenderInstitute; Fiona Williams, *Rethinking Families*, Calouste Gulbenkian Foundation 2004; Selma Sevenhuijsen, *Citizenship and the Ethic of Care*, Routledge 1998.

22. For information go to www.ic.nhs.uk/pubs/hsechildobesityupdate.

23. Stephan Collishaw, Barbara Maughan, Robert Goodman, Andrew Pickles, 'Time trends in adolescent mental health', *Journal of Child Psychology and Psychiatry and Allied Disciplines*, Nov. 2004, Vol. 45, No. 8.

24. Centre for Suicide Research, 'Youth and self harm: Perspectives', 2005, University of Oxford, http://cebmh.warne.ox.ac.uk/csr/resschools.html. See also 'Truth Hurts: Report of the National Inquiry into Self-harm among Young People', www.mentalhealth.org.uk.

25. The Nuffield Foundation, 'Seminars on Children and Families: Evidence and Implications', 2004, www.nuffieldfoundation.org/fileLibrary/pdf/2004_seminars_childern_families_adolescents_and_wellbeing001.pdf.

26. www.wales.gov.uk/subieducationtraining/content/learningcountry/foundation-consultation-e.pdf.

27. Royal College of Psychiatrists, Council Report CR84, *Institutional Abuse of Older Adults*, June 2000, www.rcpsych.ac.uk/publications/cr/cr84.htm.

28. House of Commons Health Committee, 'Elder Abuse, Second Report of Session 2003-04', Volume 1, 2004, www.publications.parliament.uk/pa/cm200304/cmselect/cmhealth/111/111.pdf.

29. Help the Aged, 'Poverty', www.helptheaged.org.uk.

30. Julia Huber and Paul Skidmore, *The New Old*, Demos 2003, www.demos.co.uk.

31. See Help the Aged, 'End-of-life care for older people', www.helptheaged.org.uk.

32. See for example, Age Concern's 2005 Position Paper, 'Age Equality', www.ageconcern.org.uk.

33. See Anna Coote, *Claiming the Health Dividend: Unlocking the Benefits of NHS Spending*, The King's Fund, www.kingsfund.org.uk. See also the comprehensive World Health Organisation framework: World Health Organisation, *Health21 – Health for All in the 21st Century*, European Health for All Series, No.6, Regional Office for Europe, Copenhagen 1999.

34. This section is based on arguments put forward by David Held in his Compass Thinkpiece on Globalisation; and in David Held, *Global Covenant, The Social Democratic Alternative to the Washington Consensus*, Polity Press 2004.

35. Christian Dustmann, Francesca Fabbri, Ian Preston, Jonathan Wadsworth, *The Local Labour Market Effects of Immigration in the UK*, Home Office Online Report 06/03, 2003.

36. Geoff Dench, Kate Gavron, Michael Young, *The New East End*, Young Foundation,

www.youngfoundation.org.uk.

37. See the Intergovernmental Panel on Climate Change, www.ipcc.ch. See also Hadley Centre, 'Stabilising climate to avoid dangerous climate change – a summary of relevant research at the Hadley Centre', January 2005, Department for Environment, Food and Rural Affairs, www.metoffice.com/research/hadleycentre/pubs/brochures/.

38. To download the report go to www.sd-commission.org.uk/pages/020506.html.

39. Jonathan Porritt, 'Hard to swallow', *Guardian*, 4 January 2006.

40. See Christian Wolmar, 'Formulating an ethical transport policy', *Renewal*, June 2005.

About Compass

Compass is the democratic left pressure group whose goal is both to debate and develop the ideas for a more equal and democratic society, then campaign and organise to help ensure they become reality. We organise regular events and conferences that provide real space to discuss policy, we produce thought-provoking pamphlets, and we encourage debate through online discussions on our website. We campaign, take positions and lead the debate on key issues facing the democratic left. We're developing a coherent and strong voice for those that believe in greater equality and democracy as the means to achieve radical social change.

We are:

- An umbrella grouping of the progressive left whose sum is greater than its parts.

- A strategic political voice – unlike thinktanks and single-issue pressure groups Compass can develop a politically coherent position based on the values of equality and democracy.

- An organising force – Compass recognises that ideas need to be organised for, and will seek to recruit, mobilise and encourage to be active a membership across the UK to work in pursuit of greater equality and democracy.

- A pressure group focused on changing Labour – but Compass recognises that energy and ideas can come from outside the party, not least from the 200,000 who have left since 1997.

- The central belief of Compass is that things will only change when people believe they can and must make a difference themselves. In the words of Gandhi, 'Be the change you wish to see in the world'.

Compass
FREEPOST LON15823
London
E9 5BR
t: 020 7463 0633
e: info@compassonline.org.uk
w: www.compassonline.org.uk

Join today and you can help change the world of tomorrow

Please contribute generously. Compass is funded solely by organisations and individuals that support our aim of greater equality and democracy. We rely heavily on individual members for funding. Minimum joining rates are suggested below. To join, simply complete and return this form to **Compass, FREEPOST LON15823, London, E9 5BR.** Paying by Standing Order or Paypal means we have a regular income to count on, consequently we are offering new members a discount for paying their membership in this way. To join by Paypal you will need to go to the Join Us section of the Compass website at www.compassonline.org.uk/join.asp.

☐ Waged (SO / Paypal) – min £27.50   ☐ Waged (Cheque / PO) – min £32.50
☐ Unwaged (SO / Paypal) – min £12.50   ☐ Unwaged (Cheque / PO) – min £17.50
☐ Organisation (i.e. CLP; think-tank; NGO) – min £42.50

Name

Address

Postcode

Telephone

Email

If you're already a Labour member what is your CLP?

Positions held

Standing order instructions

Please pay immediately by standing order to Compass' account, Lloyds TSB, 32 Oxford Street, London, W1A 2LD (a/c 2227769, sort code 30-98-71) the sum of £10 / £25 / £40 / Other £ (please delete as appropriate) and then annually, unless cancelled by me in writing.

Bank / Building Society

Bank Address

Account Name

Account Number   Sort Code

Signature

☐ I'm not eligible to be a member of the Labour Party (i.e. you're a member of another political party in the UK) and I would like to become an Associate Member of Compass (with no voting rights).